NOT SO
FAST

Thank you for being a
partner in safety.

Tim Hollister

NOT SO FAST

Parenting Your Teen Through the Dangers of Driving

TIM HOLLISTER

Foreword by Sandy Spavone, Executive Director,
National Organizations for Youth Safety

CHICAGO
REVIEW
PRESS

Published by Chicago Review Press, Incorporated
814 North Franklin Street
Chicago, Illinois 60610

ISBN 978-1-61374-872-5

Cover design: Rebecca Lown
Cover illustration: Nancy Diamond
Interior design: PerfecType, Nashville, TN

Library of Congress Cataloging-in-Publication Data

Hollister, Tim, 1957–
  Not so fast : parenting your teen through the dangers of driving / Tim Hollister;
foreword by Sandy Spavone. — 1st ed.
      p. cm.
  Includes index.
  Summary: "A new and unique approach to helping parents of teen drivers focus
on preventing dangerous situations written by a father who lost his teenage son
in a car crash"—Provided by publisher.
  ISBN 978-1-61374-872-5 (pbk.)
  1. Teenage automobile drivers. 2. Teenage automobile drivers—Attitudes.
3. Automobile driving. 4. Distracted driving. 5. Parent and teenager. 6. Traffic
safety. I. Title.

  HE5620.J8H65 2013
  629.28'30835—dc23

                          2013011953

Printed in the United States of America
5 4 3 2

For Reid

CONTENTS

FOREWORD

The National Organizations for Youth Safety (NOYS) empowers teens to take leadership roles in saving lives, preventing injuries, and promoting safe and healthy lifestyles. Traffic safety and safe teen driving are among NOYS's signature focuses.

As much as we strive to educate and encourage young people to be their own responsible guides, we recognize the critical role of parents and other adults when it comes to driving. Law enforcement, schools, and driving instructors can do only so much. As virtually every traffic safety organization recognizes, parents are essential to training and supervising teens, both before they get behind the wheel and when they do become drivers who are responsible for not only their own safety but also the public's, with whom we all share the roadway.

Because of this reality, NOYS and its more than sixty member national coalition, representing eighty million youth and adults, welcome Tim Hollister's book *Not So Fast*. All of us who have followed Tim along his journey from bereaved parent, to participant in reforming his state's teen driver law, to prolific writer and speaker about safe teen driving, welcome his compelling personal perspective, his insights into the parent-teen relationship as it affects driving, and his extraordinary efforts to fill gaps in the information available to parents and guardians of teen drivers. Simply put, Tim has done our homework for us: he has immersed himself in the data and reports, pulled out the best practices, and given us readily understood explanations of the risks of teen driving and how to avoid the most dangerous situations. His work is gratefully received by the national traffic safety community as a needed resource. Tim's willingness to turn personal tragedy into public service is a model that NOYS and its members salute, and his approach to safer teen driving is one we wholeheartedly endorse.

—Sandy Spavone
Executive Director
National Organizations for Youth Safety
Gainesville, Virginia

AUTHOR'S NOTE

Proceeds from the sale of this book will support the Reid Samuel Hollister Memorial Fund, c/o the Asylum Hill Congregational Church in Hartford, Connecticut, and traffic safety programs. Reid's Fund supports infant and toddler day care and education in the City of Hartford. Updates about contributions made from proceeds will be posted periodically on this book's website.

"Teen" primarily refers to those fifteen to twenty years old. Writing this book, I debated whether to refer to teens as "kids" or "children." I recognize, however, that every teen is different, and that while some are frighteningly unready to drive at age sixteen or seventeen (or twenty-one or twenty-five), some are level-headed and careful at fifteen. Rather than painting anyone with an unfairly broad brush, I use "teen" in both the gender-neutral and maturity-neutral senses.

Recognizing that many teens are supervised by someone other than a biological or adoptive parent, when I say "parent" I mean any adult who supervises a teen's driving (and in my model teen driving agreement, I use the term "supervising adult").

The National Highway Traffic Safety Administration avoids the term "accident" and uses "crash," to emphasize the point that every incident involving a car was preventable. I agree, and use "crash."

I have referred to statistics sparingly, and when I have, they should be regarded as highlighting a range or order of magnitude only. Fatality statistics tend to be fairly precise. Data about crashes, injuries, and costs, however, are not uniformly reported or counted; such numbers should be regarded only as indicative of trends and magnitudes.

INTRODUCTION

"Not So Fast, Young Man/Lady"

My seventeen-year-old son Reid died in a one-car crash on an interstate highway in December 2006, eleven months after receiving his license.

After the crash, I was less haunted by the feeling that I had made a terrible mistake in supervising my son's driving and more confused by the sense that I had done what parents are supposed to do, and what I saw most parents doing—and he still died.

In 2007, I was asked to serve on a task force that overhauled my state's then very lenient teen driver law. In the course of that work, I learned that during those months in 2006 I *had* been a mainstream parent: like so many others, I *had not* been well informed about the risks and dangers of teen driving—in part because much of the literature available to parents doesn't describe fully the dangers of teen driving and what parents can do to counteract them. Most articles, handbooks, and manuals, I discovered, tell parents that their job is to teach their teens the rules of the road, how to handle a car, and how to avoid hitting anything, but the literature omits or passes lightly over the many things that parents need to do *before* teens get behind the wheel.

In other words, while helping to reform my state's teen driver laws, I identified a troubling gap in the national literature, the neglect of why and how parents should manage their teen drivers day by day before they drive. This book is an effort to fill that hole.

In these pages, parents will find discussions of topics infrequently discussed in most teen driver education materials, and never pulled together in a single resource, including:

- the characteristics of teens and new drivers that make them crash-prone and, unfortunately, cannot be overcome with training and good intentions;

- why driver's ed does not produce safe drivers;

- how parent attitudes, conscious and unconscious, compound the risks;

- when a teen is ready, as opposed to eligible, to drive;

- why strict teen driver laws work;

- how to get teen drivers to heed safety warnings;

- the critical difference between purposeful driving and joyriding;

- how to negotiate and enforce a teen driving agreement that targets and preempts the riskiest situations;

- how to handle car keys;

- why passengers, including siblings, are especially dangerous;

- how to manage curfews;

- how to use traffic tickets as a teaching moment;

- the hidden safety traps of buying a car, "connected car" technology, headphones, and student transportation permission forms;

- why the price of gas is a curse and a blessing;

- why zero tolerance for electronic distractions and impaired driving is essential;
- whether teens should use a GPS;
- how to use technology to track a teen's driving;
- what high schools can do;
- supervising other people's teens; and
- the special challenges of teen driving faced by single parents and non-English-speaking households.

This is, therefore, a unique and somewhat odd book for parents of teen drivers, because it contains almost nothing about how to teach a teen to drive a car. My exclusive focus is helping parents make informed decisions about whether, when, and how their teens should drive in the first place, both initially and day to day. My purposes here are to help parents understand the real risks of teen driving, point out and counteract attitudes and assumptions that mislead parents, and empower parents to evaluate the circumstances of each day and be able to say "No" when necessary. I want to give parents the benefit of the years of homework that I have done since my son's crash so as to spare families and communities from the agony and pain that crashes, injuries, and fatalities cause.

To illustrate the misdirection of much of the literature currently available to parents, here is a Top Ten list of steps for parents of teen drivers, published by a national company:

1. Pay for more driver training than state laws require.

2. Be hands-on during the learner's permit phase.

3. Talk about safety.

4. Don't yell until you get home.

5. Review the driving session after it's over.

6. Keep track of passengers.

7. Remind your teen that driving can be dangerous.

8. Choose a car with good safety ratings.

9. Ride with your teen periodically to check on safe habits.

10. Share insurance and other costs.

The emphasis is on handling a vehicle, not intervention or management before driving to counteract risk. The underlying assumptions are that teens will begin to drive on the day they reach the legal age, and parents are virtually powerless to stop them. This typical list reinforces these attitudes; it does not prompt parents to consider each new day to be a new situation requiring a new evaluation and a new decision as to whether, when, and how their teen should drive. Missing is the theme that parents on a daily basis need to control and preempt the specific driving situations that pose the greatest risks for teens.

Why do so many manuals and articles neglect predriving supervision? We live in a car-glorifying and auto-dependent society in which getting behind the wheel is prelude to freedom and adventure, not preparation for risk. We pay money to go to the movies to see car crashes. (One advertisement for high-definition television actually boasted that "Cars smashing into little pieces look better in HD.") We anguish over the deaths of 4,500 soldiers in Iraq over several years but hardly blink at the same number of people who die on American roads every sixty days. Traffic deaths are local news, the price of our mobile society. This is the cultural backdrop for parents when their teens reach the minimum driving age and step into a grown-up world of excitement and exploration.

Parents soon to face or now immersed in this challenge, who pick up this book out of concern for their teen's safety, should understand the thankless task ahead. A parent who says "No" or "Not so fast!" to an eager teen driver is swimming against the tide. Parenting is hard and directing teens is harder, but keeping teen drivers safe may be a parent's greatest challenge; it requires, among other things, resisting pressure from both the teen's and parent's peers, counteracting an unrelenting barrage of advertising and media, inconveniencing ourselves, and recognizing the omissions, unconscious attitudes, and biases in what we read. Parents who take this book's advice—supervision first, driving second—will likely never be praised by their teens or others for saving lives or preventing injuries. They will need to be satisfied with the knowledge that they, well, went the extra mile.

Yet however daunting it may be to widen our focus when it comes to teen drivers, it is imperative that we try, because the risks of an error or mistake are injury or death, not only to a family member but also to others—passengers, other drivers, pedestrians, and bystanders. About three million teens obtain a driver's license every year in the United States, and there are annually more than thirteen million licensed drivers aged fifteen to twenty, which is 6.4 percent of the 210 million total. These teens, however, account for 14 percent of crashes. Teen driver crash rates are three times higher than those of the safest drivers, those aged thirty-five to forty-nine. In 2010, nearly two thousand teen drivers died, but three thousand "others" died in their crashes. On average, every day in the United States, approximately fourteen people die and eighty are hurt in a crash involving a teen driver.

Moreover, crashes, injuries, and fatalities know no favorites; while it is true that teen boys crash more than teen girls, crashes occur in urban, suburban, and rural communities; in affluent, middle-class, and low-income households; across ethnicities and nationalities; and to well-behaved and mature teens as well as daredevils. A news headline feed covering just ten days in mid-2011, compiled by Safe Roads 4 Teens (a group promoting national minimum standards for teen driving state laws), illustrates the geographic scope:

- Inman, South Carolina: *Teen driver killed after running off road into tree*
- Kirksville, Missouri: *Teen passenger killed in crash with sixteen-year-old driver*
- Myrtle Beach, South Carolina: *Seventeen-year-old killed, two teens injured in Spring Break crash*
- Post Falls, Idaho: *Seventeen-year-old driver killed, teen passengers injured in crash into tree*
- Reno County, Kansas: *Seventeen-year-old driver and 13-year-old brother killed in crash on way to school*

- Acton, Massachusetts: *Sixty-one-year-old man killed after being pinned by seventeen-year-old driver*
- Jonesboro, Arkansas: *Seventeen-year-old killed in crash involving train*
- North Raleigh, North Carolina: *Sixteen-year-old driver killed in single-vehicle crash*
- Marietta, Georgia: *Crash involving sixteen-year-old driver kills driver's mother.*

Can parents ignore this book and still have their teens survive injury-free into adulthood? Certainly. Hundreds of thousands of teens do. The issue is whether parents wish to roll the dice or take steps to push the odds in their favor.

Supervision before driving is every bit as important to improving the odds, to lowering crash rates, as teaching teens how to turn at a busy intersection. There are so many steps parents can take that are rarely covered in the available resources. If we can better educate thousands of parents of the three million new teens who obtain a driver's license every year to consider handling a vehicle as Step Two, to stop their overexcited teens at the door with the words "Not so fast!", and to take steps to avoid dangers and traps, we can further reduce teen driver crashes, injuries, and deaths, and their incalculable impact on families and communities.

My Story

During 2006, I was a regular, mainstream parent of a teen driver. I occasionally worried about my son's safety, but I was generally confident that the training I had given him—what state law required and the literature suggested—was sufficient.

On December 2, 2006, everything changed. My seventeen-year-old son Reid died in a one-car crash. Driving on a three-lane interstate highway that he probably had never driven before, on a dark night just after rain had stopped, and apparently traveling above the speed limit, he went too far into a curve before turning, then overcorrected, and went into a spin. While the physics of the moment could have resulted in any number of trajectories, his car hit the point of a guardrail precisely at the middle of the driver's-side door, which crushed the left side of his chest. Had the impact occurred eighteen inches forward or back, he would have survived. No alcohol, no drugs, no cell phone; his passengers were legal and he was well within the state's curfew for teen drivers. He died from speed, an unfamiliar road, and inexperience with how to handle a skid. His two passengers were injured and briefly hospitalized.

Reid's crash was a precursor to a string of horrific crashes in Connecticut. In August 2007, four teens died in one crash, and then in October, a seventeen-year-old driver killed himself, his fourteen-year-old sister, and her fifteen-year-old friend.

Reading news accounts of these other crashes, I reflected more intently on how I had—or hadn't—controlled Reid's driving. These tragedies focused me, and indeed, our entire state, on the dangers of teen driving. I found myself alternately defending my own conduct but then asking—well, if I did what I was supposed to, why was Reid dead?

Comparing other crashes to Reid's, and the actions of other parents to my own, allowed me to indulge the thought that I had been a responsible parent. We had allowed Reid to buy a safe, sensible Volvo, not a race car. I had educated myself about Connecticut's teen driving laws, made sure Reid understood them, given him more than the required twenty hours of on-the-road instruction, enrolled him in a driving school, demanded that he always wear his seat belt, revoked his driving privileges when he had disobeyed our household's rules, and even twice confiscated his car for a week or more. He drove crash-free for eleven months. Looking back, it did not seem that I had made some horrible, obvious mistake. So where did I go wrong? Would a stricter father's son still be alive?

Just a week before the first anniversary of Reid's crash, I was driving to work, listening to the morning radio news, when the announcer said that our governor was forming a Teen Safe Driving Task Force to revise Connecticut's laws, with the hope of reducing the recurring carnage on our roads. The report stated that bereaved parents would be among those asked to serve on the task force. When I got to my office, I called my state senator, my state representative, a friend who knew the Commissioner of Motor Vehicles, and a colleague who knew the governor, and asked for their help in being appointed, which I was, a week later.

Our assignment was to review the state's teen driving laws. As we proceeded, I relived how I had trained Reid and how and when

I had controlled his driving. I learned new facts about teen driving and discovered that while supervising my son, I had not been as well-informed a parent as I had thought.

In the late 1990s, Connecticut joined a growing list of states that adopted what are called "graduated driver's license" or "GDL" laws. New drivers—generally between fifteen and eighteen—face a prescribed classroom curriculum and a certain number of required driving hours supervised by an instructor, parent, or guardian. After the learner's permit stage, GDL rules delay new drivers from carrying passengers, usually for several months, and impose a curfew in the range of 9:00 PM to 1:00 AM. At eighteen, these drivers graduate to an unrestricted adult license. Beyond these basics, however, the state laws vary widely.

I learned that Connecticut in 2005–06 had one of the nation's more lenient laws, allowing teens to obtain a license as early as four months after turning sixteen, and with just twenty hours on the road and several hours of classroom instruction about speeding and drunk driving. For the first three months of being licensed, Connecticut teens could carry as passengers only a supervising driver and immediate family, but after that, they could pile their friends into their cars. The statewide curfew was midnight.

As I dug into the mountain of information made available to Task Force members, I remembered what I was thinking when I had let Reid drive. Reid's close friend Mike was a few months older, and his buddy Tom was a full year ahead; by early 2006, they both had licenses and cars. In January, Reid completed his learner's permit training and received his license. In lockstep with just about every other parent in our suburban town, my wife Ellen and I agreed to consider letting Reid buy a used car.

I took him out on lightly traveled back roads. I reviewed the state's recommended list of skills and situations to be taught to new drivers, and we spent time on each one. We practiced evasive maneuvers in an empty parking lot early on a Sunday morning. While taking driver's ed, Reid showed himself to me to be an alert, coordinated driver.

That our state had adopted GDL requirements was comforting. I assumed that the legislature, the Department of Motor Vehicles, and the police had gotten together to formulate sensible rules that, if followed, would keep Reid safe.

Finally, I cannot deny—nor, I think, can any busy parent—that having my son drive was alluringly convenient for Ellen and me, living as we do in a suburban community in which walking is usually not an option. Reid getting his license provided an extra pickup and delivery service.

Ellen and I overlaid our own rules onto state law. We were to know his destinations and his whereabouts at all times. Like all of his friends, he had a cell phone and he was under orders to check in. We made it clear repeatedly that driving was a privilege and not a right. Our rules could be modified as needed based on particular circumstances, such as our judgment that he had not gotten enough sleep. Reid understood that when he arrived home, I would be waiting for him and I would conduct my own interrogation, checking for coherence and sobriety. On a few occasions when he missed his curfew, I confiscated his keys. Although I don't recall discussing it overtly with Reid, I think he also understood that I was regularly inspecting every nook and crevice in his car—just like his room—and I was keeping an eye on his mileage.

As I let the reins out on Reid's driving—longer periods in the car by himself, longer distances, driving at night or in bad weather—I relived my own driving experience and I wondered if I had inadvertently conveyed any bad habits to my son. To my relief, he continued to show himself to be a calm, coordinated driver, with a good sense of the position of the vehicle on the road. No news became good news.

In April, when Reid had been licensed for three months, an officer pulled him over for a moving violation, crossing two lanes without signaling. According to Reid, the violation was questionable. The fine was $204, which Reid paid from his own savings account.

As the summer wore on, I became concerned about Reid revving the engine—it was the only way he could make his clunky used car seem cool. I was not particularly alarmed but more concerned that he would rev the engine while on the road into an excessive speed and find himself with another expensive ticket. In late September, he was cited for driving 42 mph in a 25 mph zone. Because this was his second moving violation before turning eighteen, he not only incurred a fine but had to attend a driver retraining class at the Department of Motor Vehicles. He signed up for the last possible day: December 2. I suppose that subconsciously I appreciated that teenage drivers are inexperienced and not yet mentally mature. Yet I did not personally know any family that had lost a teenage driver in a crash, I had survived my teen years, I knew my son, I had trained him, and I assumed that the state's laws would keep him safe.

But that's not what happened; Reid died six hours before he was due to attend the DMV retraining.

In my first two months serving on the Task Force, I sifted through a mountain of statistics, analyses, and reports and found that teen driving is more dangerous than I had understood while parenting Reid, and that Connecticut's GDL laws were weaker than I had realized. I had allowed Reid to drive in situations that were much more perilous than I had thought.

In addition to research, subcommittee meetings, and Task Force sessions, I met and spoke at length with police, psychologists, doctors, nurses, prosecutors, judges, school principals, driving instructors, social workers, traffic safety officials, and other bereaved parents. As I began to read and listen to facts and proposals for improving the laws, a question popped into my head and then repeated itself week after week, each time a bit louder and more tinged with disbelief: *Why had I not learned all of this earlier?* This was a maddening combination of outward—"Why didn't anyone tell me?"—and inward—"Why didn't I better educate myself?" Why had I not been more conservative in my decisions about Reid's driving? Like so many other parents, had I been seduced by the convenience of having another driver in the house?

During the first six months of 2008, the Task Force became my near obsession. We traveled to high schools across the state and appeared on statewide television. I was interviewed on WCBS radio about my re-education.

Within four months—a quickness rare in the world of public policy—the Task Force recommended, the governor endorsed, and the legislature adopted stricter rules for sixteen- and seventeen-year-olds: doubling of the required hours during the learner's permit stage; moving the curfew from midnight back to 11:00 PM; prohibiting teen drivers from transporting anyone other than parents, guardians, and siblings until licensed for a full year; suspending licenses, starting at thirty days, for moving violations (instead of just monetary fines); providing faster court prosecutions and driver retraining sessions; requiring a parent or guardian to attend a two-hour safety class with each teen during driver's ed; requiring all passengers of teen drivers to wear seat belts; and allowing law enforcement to confiscate a teen's license and impound the car for forty-eight hours if the situation warranted.

After the governor signed the bill before a bank of TV cameras and a crowd of legislators in the sun-splashed courtyard of a high school, I calculated the difference that these new laws would have made in the life of my son. Had the 2008 law been in effect in 2006, Reid would have had double the hours of required on-the-road training; Ellen or I would have attended a safety class with him while he had his learner's permit; his first moving violation (the double lane change) would have earned him a thirty-day license suspension; his second violation would have cost him his license for sixty days, plus a fine for license reinstatement; he would have taken his driver retraining class sooner; and he would not have been allowed to have the passengers who were with him when he crashed. The new laws were too late but not too little.

When all of this settled in my mind, there was no doubt that I had to find a way to communicate my new perspectives to other parents. It was undeniably true that I had not fully appreciated how dangerous teen driving is in the best of circumstances or how risk escalates in a variety of predictable and therefore controllable situations. Having read all of the available literature and consulted the mainstream sources, I started to think that parents need better information.

And so, in October 2009, I started speaking out, by launching "From Reid's Dad," my national blog for parents of teen drivers. Eighteen months and fifty posts later, I had the basis for this book.

Why There Is No Such Thing as a Safe Teen Driver

In 2009, the *Wall Street Journal* began a series of personal advice columns written jointly by its San Francisco Bureau Chief Steve Yoder and his teenage son Isaac. In their columns, father Steve offered advice to Isaac about how to succeed in college, while Isaac counseled his younger brother about how to succeed in high school. In one letter, Isaac told his younger sibling: "Obtain your driver's license early and make use of it. It will extend your boundaries and your freedom."

It's hard to argue with that advice. Getting a driver's license is a major step from childhood to young adulthood. Having a license allows teens to travel to school and extracurricular activities, get and hold a job, explore new places, broaden their knowledge of geography, and gain new perspectives on where and how people live and work.

Without knowing, I assume that Isaac's experience in getting his license was uneventful and a considerable source of pride to his parents, and probably a convenience in a family with a younger sibling who regularly needed transportation.

So, with all these allures and benefits embedded in a teen getting a driver's license, why did Isaac's advice to his younger brother make me shudder?

Because, unfortunately, there is no such thing as a safe teen driver. While getting a license "early" creates opportunities for education, employment, and exploration, it also elevates the risk of a disabling or fatal crash.

Why are all teens, including the levelheaded, risk-aware, and well-trained ones, at risk? There are four reasons:

- the human brain does not fully develop until we reach our early or mid-twenties, and the last part of the brain to mature is the prefrontal cortex, the part that provides judgment and restraint and counterbalances the already developed part that creates desire, excitement, and risk-taking;

- driving requires the continuous evaluation of hundreds of ever-changing factors and circumstances, and thus experts say that it takes three to five *years* of experience to become familiar and comfortable with the myriad situations that drivers encounter, not the twenty to one hundred *hours* that most states require for a teen to obtain a license;

- new drivers generally look at the perimeter of their car and focus on not hitting anything, rather than looking down the road where they would see developing situations and dangers; and

- we train teens on local, familiar roads, but then driving inevitably takes them to highways in unfamiliar places, so they must learn to drive while also trying to navigate.

Thus, teen drivers, no matter how well-intentioned, trustworthy, respectful, schooled in safe driving laws, and thoroughly trained in how to safely operate a car, *do not have and cannot obtain* the essential elements of a safe driver: a brain that quickly and accurately perceives and responds to risk and danger; judgment to deal with a variety of fast-moving and ever-changing situations that every driver faces; the confidence to look ahead down the road instead of focusing on the car's perimeter; the experience to concentrate on what the car's next maneuvers will be instead of how to execute them; and enough time behind the wheel so that most driving is with a familiar vehicle on a familiar road. These characteristics take considerable time, which cannot be cut short or accelerated.

The slow-to-mature brain is the most problematic characteristic; the teen brain is simply constrained physically and chemically. The prefrontal cortex—which provides the connectivity (a.k.a. wiring) that enables organization, planning, interpretation, and inhibition—is the last part of the brain to develop, typically being complete around age twenty-five. The lobe that generates emotion is in place years earlier, thus accounting for teens' penchant for reacting more from emotion than reason.

This phenomenon also results from the brain's generation of chemicals known as neurotransmitters. One chemical called dopamine stimulates needs and desires for excitement, and another, serotonin, alerts the body to risk and prompts defensive actions. In the brains of teens, dopamine outweighs serotonin. As one doctor has explained, dopamine is "the gas" and serotonin is "the brakes," so teens are mentally more gas and less brake.

Applied to driving, these twin realities mean that teen drivers do not recognize hazards or assess the risk or danger in a car's maneuver or in a complex traffic situation, and so their reactions are often late and their decisions poor. Only the completion of physical development of the brain and the balancing of the chemical proportions can overcome this barrier to safe driving.

It is important to note that "safe" is a relative term. All driving is risky. Drivers aged thirty-five to forty-nine have the lowest crash rates. Their brains are fully developed, their combination of experience and good reflexes is the best of any driver group, and they have the greatest personal and professional reasons to drive safely. Yet middle-aged drivers are *safer*, not safe. Teen drivers are at significantly *greater* risk.

So yes, a driver's license can help a teen with school, a job, and knowledge of the world. But these allures should not distract or blind us from the facts that the risks of teen driving are substantial and largely unchangeable except through years of physical growth, emotional maturity, and much more experience than state laws typically require for a teen to get a license.

3

Baseline Dangers and Higher Risk Factors

John Rosemond, the parenting-advice columnist, once posed this question to parents of teens: "Would you allow your son or daughter to participate in an activity that had a one in 10,000 chance of death?" To a person, the parents said no.

Then Rosemond revealed that the activity he was talking about was driving.

The government, insurance companies, and highway safety analysts and advocates have collected mountains of data about driving. The numbers they report vary somewhat, but in round numbers there are approximately thirteen million teen drivers (ages fifteen to twenty) in the United States, and in recent years (2006–2010) about 3,000 teen drivers have died and 200,000 have been injured each year in crashes. These numbers equate to ballparks of a 1/4,300 chance of death for teen drivers and a 1/65 chance of a serious injury.

As Mark Twain implied when he wrote about "lies, damned lies, and statistics," these averages are misleading. As the saying goes, if

17

I have one foot in an ice bucket and one on a bed of hot coals, on average I am comfortable, but that's not the whole story. Applied to teen driving, these calculations of average hide the fact that even the best-trained, law-abiding teens are at risk (maybe Rosemond picked one in 10,000 to represent the most careful teen drivers) but there are several behaviors while driving that elevate the risk far above these scary-enough-as-is averages.

Teen driving always involves what experts call "baseline dangers." As noted earlier, the brains of teens do not yet fully appreciate risk and danger, and teens lack the experience and judgment essential to driving. Safe driving takes years, and new drivers are learning simultaneously to drive, navigate, and extend their vision up the road. Thus, if we prepared a safety scale for teen drivers and assigned a label to each tier, the lowest, safest level would be "At Risk," not "Safe."

The point is that for teens, the dangers start at "at risk" and go up from there. It is impossible to rank these risk-elevating factors or assign them point totals, because each factor has its own variations and levels—speed and blood alcohol level, for example. We do have approximations, however, such as the recent study concluding that drivers (of any age) who text are twenty-three times more likely to crash than those who don't. These are factors that spike the punchbowl, so to speak:

- drugs, alcohol, and anything that impairs reflexes and judgment;
- distracted driving (texting, cell phones, iPods, other electronic devices);
- speeding;
- passengers;
- failure to use seat belts;
- bad weather;
- night driving;
- impulsiveness and aggressive behavior;

- Attention Deficit Disorder or any similar condition; and
- fatigue.

These factors make the averages discussed above virtually meaningless. If the safest teen driver is at risk and the average teen driver has a one in 4,300 chance of dying behind the wheel, these higher-risk factors push the odds of a serious crash into a "waiting to happen" category. Then, if a teen driver combines one or more of these higher risk factors, such as speeding and passengers or a cell phone and alcohol, the relevance of these averages diminishes even further because the likelihood of a debilitating crash goes even higher: alcohol and texting, speeding and passengers, drug use and no seat belts, and so on.

Teens with Attention Deficit Disorder and Attention Deficit Hyperactivity Disorder require an additional level of supervision. Distractibility, an inability to focus for lengthy time periods, and an elevated tendency to take risks are, of course, at odds with safe driving. Many teens can control ADD/ADHD behaviors with medication, and thus it is essential that teens with these conditions take the proper dosage at a proper time before driving. There are some teens, however, with more severe symptoms who simply should not drive at all.

To bring the point back to Mr. Rosemond: bear in mind and explain to your teens that the statistical average likelihood of their getting into a serious crash is high to begin with, but there are behaviors and choices that can transform the average risk of a crash into a near certainty.

The baseline dangers also have a time-of-year element: *twice as many teens die on the roads during the summer months as during the rest of the year.* Traffic safety agency reports for the past several years contain these sobering statistics:

- from May through August, fatalities in crashes involving teen drivers average nearly sixteen per day, as compared to just under nine per day during the other eight months;
- six of the seven deadliest days of the year occur between May and August; and

- on the single deadliest day of the year, usually in late May (the height of prom season), the average number of deaths (twenty-five) is three times the level of the least deadly (we can't say "safest") day, which is just above eight.

Figuring out why there are more fatalities in the summer months is not difficult. It is simply due to the difference between purposeful and recreational driving, as pointed out in chapter 10. When teens have a destination, a route, a timetable, and a consequence for not arriving on time, they are far more likely to arrive safely than when they are "joyriding," that is, driving for fun. Guess which type of driving increases substantially during the late spring and summer months? Proms, trips to the beach, the mall, the movies, or to a concert are all recreational driving because there is no consequence for being late.

The steps described in this book that parents need to take to supervise their teen drivers are always needed, but especially from May through August.

"My Kid Is Very Responsible!"

As the statewide task force on which I served began to consider stricter GDL requirements in early 2008, e-mails from both parents and students began pouring into a website set up by the Department of Motor Vehicles. While many parents expressed support for stricter laws, some were opposed, and some were outraged. I began to realize that parents, by definition, are the ones who survived their teen driving years, and some made that fact the basis of their opinion about what the state's law should be. They raised objections, such as:

> I don't want to see my children punished with severe restrictions just because they are teenagers.

> It should be a parent's choice if they want their new driver to be in the car with another person. Another person makes the new driver better because they are another set of eyes.

While the intention is to reduce the incidence of horrific accidents that maim or kill multiple teens, the fact is that teens need to rely on each other for transportation, and these laws would cause a huge inconvenience.

If teens cannot carry passengers then they are forced to drive alone, which wastes gas and money and puts more cars on the road, which is bad for air quality.

Teenagers have very busy lives.

The fact is that our children have to grow up, and to do that they have to make mistakes, and some of those mistakes will be fatal.

Candidly, these e-mails helped convince task force members that we needed a stronger law.

More recently, I saw a letter to a newspaper that said:

If our country were as small as most European countries, making kids wait until they're 18 to get their licenses might be more reasonable. Europe has better mass transit. But to expect parents to drive their little darlings to and from school, to and from work, and to and from all social activities is not reasonable.

Do you agree? Does this parent's attitude sound similar to your thought process? I hope not. The author did not appear to be aware that if the minimum driving age were based on the science of brain development rather than tradition and political pushback from parents, the starting age would be in the range of twenty-one to twenty-five, not sixteen to eighteen. This writer also placed convenience ahead of safety; the words signal an impatience with teens not getting their licenses because of the imposition on parents' schedules. The implication is a willingness to force a teen who may not be ready to drive to do so, because "It's time to grow up."

Parental oversight can also be hindered by defensiveness. Some consider their teen's driving a reflection of their attentiveness and performance as a parent. Any suggestion that the teen is not a good driver constitutes a personal insult. The thought that our own teens are more responsible than others, because we are ourselves, can get in the way of clear thinking about how best to control driving.

We can divide parent attitudes into dos and don'ts: Don't let your personal convenience get in the way of safety. Don't be desensitized by popular culture and entertainment and the news media to the dangers of driving. Don't be lulled into false security, believing that a responsible teen who has taken driver's education and passed the state's road test is a safe driver. Don't be reckless or indifferent.

What should a parent's attitudes be?

- Understand and accept the dangers of teen driving as your baseline.

- Be willing to say no to your teens, especially at three stages: (1) when they want to get a learner's permit but your heart and head tell you that they are not ready yet; (2) when they want to graduate from learner's permit to licensed solo driving and you have the same fear; and (3) when your licensed driver, day by day, runs into circumstances, such as fatigue or stress, that counsel you to say "No driving *today*."

- Use your parent power to withhold car keys when you need to.

- Be vigilant day by day for the situations described in this book: purposeful driving vs. joyriding, managing curfews, prohibiting passengers, prohibiting texting, not buying a car for a teen's own use, using a traffic ticket as a teaching moment, signing and following a teen driving agreement.

- When in doubt, err on the side of being conservative. There is simply no room for error when we manage teen drivers.

- Approach parenting your teen driver with the attitude of working together to make safety the top priority.

It may be useful to think of parenting teen drivers on a scale: reckless, indifferent, ignorant, informed but not proactive, willing but misinformed, informed and proactive. Strive to be in this final category.

What Driver's Ed Isn't

W hen I refer to "driver's ed," I mean all types of teen driver training and education, whether provided by parents, guardians, relatives, other adults supervising drivers, high schools, or commercial driving schools.

Parents who delve into the voluminous research about what is and is not effective in reducing crash rates among teen drivers will find this confusing conclusion: *there is little evidence showing that driver education for teens reduces crash rates among teen drivers.* Federal highway safety agencies, state motor vehicle departments, insurance company associations, and university transportation institutes that have researched this issue have all reached the same conclusion.

So does this research mean that parents are wasting their money, and teens are wasting their time, when they enroll in driver's ed? The answer is certainly no—but beneath the surface of this seemingly contradictory answer lies a critical reality about safe teen driving.

Obviously, teens need to learn the rules of the road and how to operate a car safely, and how to pass the state's written and road skills test to obtain a license. Without question, the more hours they spend behind the wheel receiving supervised training, the better drivers they will be when they begin driving solo. The research and the data absolutely do not imply that we should not train teen drivers before licensing them.

The primary problems are that (1) driver's ed does not overcome the reasons why there is no such thing as a safe teen driver (chapter 2); and (2) the typical driver education course provides thirty to forty-five hours of classroom lectures and six to twenty hours on the road, which is too little to do anything to lower crash rates. Driver's ed is necessary but not sufficient to create a safe driver. (One public policy consequence of this reality is that state laws that allow earlier licensing for teens who take a driver education course mislead parents into thinking that the course provides a safety benefit.)

The research demonstrating that driver's ed does not reduce teen driver crash rates does not mean that commercial driving schools and other driver education programs are worthless. The data, however, provide the clear lesson that parents should not assume that a teen who has taken driver's ed and passed is an experienced or safe driver. *A graduate of driver's ed who becomes a newly licensed teen driver is a beginner.* Beginners have the highest crash rates. A driver's license is government's permission to begin to participate—in a dangerous activity.

The ABCs of GDL (Graduated Driver Licensing)

Every parent of a teen driver should understand the basic elements of Graduated Driver Licensing laws and the critical facts now proven by mountains of statistical research, nationwide: they target the baseline dangers of teen driving, they work, and the stricter the law, the better the results.

The core idea of a GDL system is three-stage licensing: a learner's permit phase, a period of restrictions on unsupervised driving, and finally a full license. The specific components of GDL laws are:

- a specified minimum age at which a teen may obtain a learner's permit and then a license;

- required hours of on-the-road training that a learner's permit holder must receive from a driving instructor, parent, guardian, or supervising adult before moving up to a license (often called a "holding" period);

- passenger restrictions once the teen obtains a license;
- a curfew (morning start time, evening deadline) for teen drivers being on the road;
- rules about electronic devices and texting (which are often stricter than for older drivers);
- seat belt rules, such as requiring every passenger to be buckled when a teen is driving; and
- monetary fines, license suspensions, license revocations, or some combination, for first-time and repeat offenders.

It's important to understand that each state establishes its own motor vehicle laws, including teen driver laws. The federal government generally does not intrude on this state power, the exceptions being withholding federal funds for highway construction and maintenance in order to incentivize states to follow a minimum national standard, such as establishing age twenty-one as the minimum for purchase of alcohol, and making seat belts mandatory. Thus, at this time, although the federal government in 2012 approved a program that will provide financial incentives for states to adopt GDL laws that meet specified minimum standards, there is no federal GDL. The other critical fact is that state GDL laws vary widely, with a few states having minimal rules and only a few, such as New Jersey, featuring strict requirements throughout their statutes.

Several national organizations regularly track, compare, and rate state teen driver laws, such as the Governors Highway Safety Association, www.ghsa.org (the "Survey of States" website section); and the Insurance Institute for Highway Safety, www.iihs.org. State motor vehicle department websites, of course, explain that state's legal requirements. Parents should determine how strict their own state's GDL program is, because the stricter a state's law, the more help a parent has in controlling a teen driver, and the more lenient a state's law, the more responsibility the parent has to impose rules over and above the state's.

GDL laws work because they take direct aim at the most prominent causes of teen driver crashes and fatalities: they delay the issuance of learner's permits and licenses; restrict passengers; require education about impaired driving, electronic devices, and texting; keep teens off the road late at night and early in the morning; establish seat belt rules; and specify penalties for violations; or some combination of these. Put another way, these laws allow teens to gain on-the-road experience under less challenging conditions and situations, such as supervised, daytime operation. Fully documented research shows that as GDL systems are adopted and strengthened, crash rates, injuries, and fatalities decline.

Serving on my state's task force, however, I learned three political realities about GDL laws. First, the most vocal opposition to stronger GDL programs comes from parents—those who view teen drivers through the lens of their own convenience, the misplaced attitude that their well-behaved teen will never crash the car, or the misguided notion that the way to help teens grow up is to let them drive. Second, political change for the most part occurs incrementally, with small or modest changes in a given year being easier for legislators to approve. As a result, in states whose GDL requirements, based on current research, are well below the standards specified in the new federal financial incentive program, bringing each state's teen driver law up to even a minimally acceptable standard will likely take years. Finally (this will come as a shock), politicians react to news events. In my state, it took the deaths of seven teens in a three-month period in 2007 to create a public outcry that induced our governor and legislature to convene a task force and rewrite our laws. Sadly, for those advocating tougher teen driver laws in their state, it often takes a tragedy to focus attention and create public support and political will.

When Should a Teen Start Driving?

Should the minimum age for licensing teen drivers be fifteen, sixteen, seventeen, eighteen, or even higher? This issue has been debated for years by legislators and traffic safety professionals across the country. It's important to recognize, however, that the question itself can mislead parents.

When state governments adopt teen driving laws they establish minimums, what lawyers call "bright line standards," meaning that whether or not the rule is good public policy, at least it is clear: if the minimum age is sixteen, and your teen is fifteen years and 364 days old, she cannot get a learner's permit or a license, but if she is sixteen years and one day old, she can. Put another way, teen driver laws tell parents and teens when teens become eligible to apply for a permit or a license; the birth certificate does the rest.

Thus, when states set a minimum age, they establish a single rule for every teen and every family. Across most of the United States, state laws allow teens to obtain learner's permits when they turn fifteen or sixteen and a so-called restricted, provisional, or junior license a few months later. When the Task Force on which I served met in 2008 to revise our laws, some argued that if the minimum age were raised to seventeen or eighteen, it would actually be harder for many parents to train their teens to drive, because so many leave the house around age eighteen, to attend college or to work. On the other hand, New Jersey has established a minimum licensing age of seventeen, which has reduced crash and fatality rates.

However, asking what the statewide minimum should be is a deceiving question; *the proper focus should be at what age your teen should be allowed to drive, regardless of what state law says.* Some commentators call this the "age of responsibility," to distinguish it from the "age of eligibility."

Parents need to be aware that each state's minimum driving age is influenced by politics (legislators vying for support and votes of parents); tradition (the minimum age has been about sixteen for a generation); culture (America romanticizes its automobiles); and simplicity (governments need rules that are easy to administer). But in no way, shape, or form are minimum driving age laws based on traffic science or traffic safety data showing that even some teens can safely drive at age sixteen, seventeen, or eighteen. In fact, these ages are directly *contrary* to what science, crash data, and numerous teen driver studies now tell us. If teen driver laws strictly followed science and data, the minimum driving age would be twenty-two to twenty-five.

So, parents, do not be misled: state law may say that your son or daughter is now old enough to drive, but in your judgment, is he or she ready to drive safely? The factors to assess are:

- appreciation of risk (is your teen a risk taker?);
- emotional maturity (can your teen handle the stress of driving?);
- physical maturity (is your teen coordinated enough to handle a car, strong enough to change a tire?); and
- fear (will the dangers of driving overwhelm your teen's driver training?).

Every parent needs to make these evaluations. Those who don't are sidestepping a crucial responsibility. In this calculation, the two factors that have no place whatsoever are the convenience of having another driver in the house, and pressure from peers—yours or your teen's. Just because your state's teen driver laws allow your teen to obtain a license does not mean that the state has determined that that age is safe for most teens; it is up to you to be the extra filter in the process, to decide whether your teen is ready to learn to be, and become, a responsible driver. Forget the legal age and focus on the age of responsibility. Your state may have a law, *but you have a veto.*

There is one more wrinkle to the minimum age issue: several studies now show that when states adopt stricter laws for sixteen- and seventeen-year-olds, some teens simply wait until their eighteenth birthday to get their license, so they don't have to go through the hassles of the laws that apply to sixteen- and seventeen-year-olds. Though the data are not yet clear, there is some evidence that crash rates for eighteen- and nineteen-year-olds have increased as a result. In any event, the primary determinants of safety for new teen drivers are not biological age but brain development and driving experience. The step-by-step introduction of driving privileges is more important than imposing rules on particular birthdays. The public policy issue, then, is whether to extend GDL laws past age eighteen. A handful of states have adopted rules that reach these older new drivers, but undoubtedly regulating driving among eighteen and nineteen-year-olds is more complicated: Many of them are out of the house, either for school or employment; they have greater legal rights and protections, including privacy; they are more likely to need a car for economic reasons; and they can vote. Perhaps the main point is that *there is nothing magic about eighteen when it comes to driving and safety.* It happens to be a significant number in our legal system, but it is not a dividing line for measuring driver safety.

Acting Like an
Air Traffic Controller

I n early 2011, the national media reported on air traffic controllers falling asleep on the job. Thinking of teen drivers as pilots and parents as air traffic controllers is not a bad analogy, actually. Parents should consider every time their teen proposes to get behind the wheel as the equivalent of a pilot wanting to fly a plane. Teens should be required to file a flight plan and get permission from the tower—you—before taking off.

The elements of this flight plan should include what a pilot would consider essential:

- Destination: Where exactly are you going? (Pilots don't estimate—they need precision.)

- Route: What directions will get you there, and are there safety concerns associated with any of them?

- Time of day: When are you leaving, and are there any safety issues implicit in your timetable (for example, night driving)?

- Equipment readiness: Do you have sufficient fuel, and is your equipment maintained and safe?

- Communications plan: When and how will you report to your guardian when you arrive at your destination, report a problem or delay, and report when you are about to return home?

- Passengers: Who will be with you, where will they sit, and how will you ensure that they don't distract you?

- Contingency plan: What will be your alternate route if the intended one is blocked or otherwise not available?

- Return trip: Do you have a set departure time, route, timetable, and passenger list (same considerations as the first leg of the trip)?

- Mental state: Are you well rested and alert?

- Overall: Are you ready to undertake this responsibility?

Only when each of these items has been satisfactorily planned should your teen be cleared for departure.

Sound silly? Overkill? If you think so, I respectfully suggest that you return to the dangers of teen driving. The risks of an unprepared pilot flying are not unlike those facing a teen driver. The margin for error is very small, and the risks are enormous.

A significant benefit of thinking of teen driving like a pilot's flight plan is that it should help you and your teen focus on the difference between driving with a destination, purpose, and timetable, and joy-riding (more on this in chapter 10). Pilots don't take joyrides, in the sense that they don't fly a plane "just to go hang out with friends." Even when flying is recreational, a pilot prepares and files a plan.

Planning the route is especially important, for a pilot and for a teen. *New drivers should not be allowed to drive a route that a supervising adult does not know.* Supervising adults should consider whether there are locations on that route that are potentially unsafe, such as a curve at the end of a straightaway; a left lane merge onto a busy highway; a stretch of three- or four-lane highway where drivers are constantly changing lanes to get to exits; places with poor visibility; unfamiliar roundabouts with multiple entry points, and so on. Parents should instruct teens to take a route that avoids these more dangerous places, or at least warn them what they will face in that location.

Will this air controller routine feel a bit less necessary when your teen is on his or her one-hundredth "flight" and has gotten the checklist down quite well? Yes. When you and your teen have spent perhaps a year in this mode, taking every driving episode so seriously that each of the steps listed above becomes automatic, will you need to maintain this level of detail? Probably not. There will come a time when it will not be as critical to be as deliberate and mechanical as suggested above. But the likelihood that your teens will get to this later stage will be substantially increased if, as they begin to drive, you work with them to treat every situation as if they are pilots preparing to fly a plane, and your supervision resembles that of a certified flight controller—one who is awake and on the job at all times.

Negotiating and Enforcing a Teen Driving Agreement

A teen driving agreement (TDA) is a written, signed agreement between a teen driver and his or her parent or guardian that acknowledges the risks and dangers of driving, states clear rules for the teen driver's conduct for a defined time period after the teen is first licensed, and establishes consequences for a violation of those rules. One of the primary purposes of a TDA is to ensure that parents and teens have detailed, calm, and candid talks about when and how permission to drive will be granted and the consequences of misconduct *before* a teen starts driving, instead of after a crash, a violation, or other misconduct.

A TDA is not a:

- legally binding agreement that a parent/guardian or teen may enforce in court;

- substitute for on-the-road driver training;

- reason to allow a teen who is not yet ready to drive safely to get behind the wheel;

- basis for a parent or guardian to be less vigilant; or
- defense against liability if the parent is sued.

It is important to understand that a TDA is not a legal document. By no means does this distinction detract from the importance of entering into one, but everyone should understand what the agreement is and isn't.

Online, you will find, most prominently, Allstate Insurance's contract, www.allstateteendriver.com. Allstate has pioneered parent-teen agreements and through its national advertising campaign, including full-page ads in major newspapers, promoted them heavily. In addition, most of the major insurance companies have their own versions, as does nearly every state motor vehicle department website. There are several "dot.com" websites that sell model parent-teen contracts for about $20 per download, with driving agreements being among dozens of subjects available. (Why any parent would pay for one of these is unclear to me; plenty of free ones are available.)

I have reviewed dozens of agreements online, and would caution against models with these characteristics:

- bare-bones wording that doesn't acknowledge or address the substantial risks and dangers of teen driving;

- lack of reference to the most recent research about how the brains of teens underappreciate risk, and to the huge dangers of texting and electronic devices;

- language that tries to sound legal and binding but instead sows confusion ("The party of the first part, hereinafter called the 'Teen Driver' . . .");

- pages of upfront instructions, categories of violations, and "special" notes that carve out major exceptions;

- statements of unclear or vague consequences ("If I do x-y-z, I *may* lose my license for *a few* days . . .");

- absence of a defined timeframe or an intention to renegotiate only weeks after signing;

- provisions that are simply contrary to the published research, such as those that only prohibit passengers "at night" (numerous studies show that passengers increase risks at any hour of the day, and one of the most unsafe hours of the day is immediately after school lets out); and

- coverage of non-driving-related subjects, such as homework, grades, allowance, "life responsibilities," household chores, parental respect, firearms, lending the car to another driver, and so forth.

Signing a TDA should never distract a parent from the essential question of whether a teen is ready to be licensed or should get behind the wheel in particular circumstances. A TDA is an upfront agreement about driving conduct but should not allow an unready teen to drive.

There are a number of keys to negotiating a sound TDA:

Mutual Objectives. In their classic book *Getting to Yes*, Roger Fisher and William Ury advise that negotiation of any agreement should focus on achieving a mutual objective, interests instead of positions, and "separating the people from the problem." For a TDA, this means starting with the mind-set that the ultimate, mutual goal is the safety of the driver, passengers, and everyone who shares the road with the teen. A TDA should be a cooperative process that ends in achievement, not victory.

The Need to Compromise. Introducing the idea of a TDA to your teen and then starting the negotiation will unleash conflicting forces. As a parent—that is, the person with the keys and thus the power— you must make it clear that negotiating and signing an agreement is a nonnegotiable part of your teen being allowed to drive, but then you need to show your teen your willingness to be reasonable, to listen, and to accommodate his or her viewpoint whenever you can. Put another way, an agreement is most likely to be followed if both parties give up something substantive; a common definition of a good compromise is a deal that no one likes but everyone accepts as the best that can be done. Therefore, as a parent, you should insist on an agreement but not dictate every term, and remember that an important part of a TDA is the very act of discussing safety issues with your teen.

The Need to Customize. Every family and every teen face different circumstances. If parents are divorced, or a guardian is in charge of the teen's conduct, the negotiation may be more difficult than if two parents are present, informed, and fully engaged by the process. If the teen has a job that requires driving, this reality will need to be accommodated. Rules and exceptions also will vary for rural, suburban, and urban areas, and based on family financial circumstances.

Motivation. When explaining to your teen why an agreement is essential, mention at least these reasons:

- driving can cause injury, death, damage, and financial liability, and can even result in a criminal conviction;
- even though state government will allow teens to drive before age eighteen, parents remain legally and financially responsible for their teen's driving;
- listing the punishment of misconduct helps deter it; and
- deciding on what will result from bad driving is better done before the teen starts to drive, rather than in the aftermath of a crash or a ticket.

Principles and Facts. A TDA should start with a list of agreed-upon facts and principles, including why teen driving is dangerous, why the teen and parent(s) are signing the agreement, and the fact that each supervising adult must be a role-model driver.

When to Negotiate and Sign. My recommendation is to negotiate and sign the agreement when the teen obtains a learner's permit, so that both the teen and supervising adult(s) can keep the proposed terms in mind as the teen progresses through driving instruction. Then revisit, modify if necessary, and finalize when the teen obtains a driver's license.

Term of the Agreement. Most model agreements available on the Internet have no time period or are based on an unstated assumption that the agreement lasts until the driver turns eighteen, when most states relax or remove restrictions on such matters as passengers and curfews. Conversely, a few models treat the initial agreement as something to be renegotiated periodically. The agreement should be in effect for a minimum of one year from when the teen becomes a licensed driver (that is, authorized to drive solo) or until the teen's eighteenth birthday, whichever is *longer*, with no reference to renegotiation. Thus, if the teen is licensed while he or she is age seventeen, the agreement should remain in place for one full year even if this extends it past the eighteenth birthday. The teen should understand that the agreement will be changed only if state laws change or the family or teen undergoes a major life change (parents separating or divorcing, a geographic move, injury or disability, change in economic circumstances, and so on).

Consistency with State Law. Every provision needs to be consistent with or stricter than state law. Thus, if the state's curfew is 11:00 PM, the agreement can set an earlier but not later time.

Addition to State Law. Suppose your teen receives a ticket and a conviction that will result in the state motor vehicle department suspending his license. Must he accept the suspension in your agreement *and* the state's penalty? I think so. First, the police and state agencies can take weeks or months to process a license suspension; only a parent can invoke the suspension when it is most needed, which is immediately. Second, the teen should understand that parents/families and the police/state government have different interests in safe teen driving, each important. As a matter of deterring misconduct, the teen should understand that one violation may result in two suspensions.

"Suspension" Not "Consequence." Many contracts on the Internet use the word "consequence" to describe what happens after a violation, but this word is so often used for young children that I think "suspension" is better. This word also reinforces that driving is a privilege, not a right.

No Driving, or No Solo Driving? A critical decision is whether the teen will lose his or her privilege of driving solo, or driving altogether. In other words, will the consequence be to revert to the learner's permit mode, where the teen may still drive but only with the parent or guardian in the car? There are two schools of thought here. One is that teens need on-the-road experience, and suspending all driving interferes with continued training. Another is that misconduct should result in no driving at all. Also factored here is how the teen, under a suspension, gets to school, a job, or activities. Some parents will say, "You lost your license, you find a ride." The teen might try to find a ride with a peer that violates the state's passenger restrictions. I can't prescribe an answer here, but I urge parents to think through this issue.

Counting Days. Understand how you will calculate a suspension. One way is to specify the exact number of days, start Day 1 when the suspension is imposed (and hopefully, agreed upon), and count twenty-four-hour periods starting then. Thus, if the violation occurs Saturday night, you discuss the situation Sunday morning, and your teen gives up his license on Sunday at noon for the agreed-on seven days, the suspension ends at noon the following Sunday.

Curfew Exceptions. Most state curfew laws have exceptions, such as for school-related activities or employment. If your teen will be invoking one of these exceptions (for example, he has a job that ends after the curfew), write in how this will be handled.

Finances. A TDA is a good place for a basic statement regarding what part of driving costs will be paid by the parent and by the teen.

Parent Override. Teens may balk at this suggestion, which in a way undermines the purpose of a written agreement, but parents are ultimately responsible for the safety of their teens. Supervision of teen driving requires judgment, and circumstances can arise in the life of a teen such that driving will be unsafe. A parent needs to have on-the-spot suspension authority, and a TDA should recognize this. If, for example, a teen has gone on a school field trip, arrived home at 3:00 AM, and wants to drive somewhere at 7:00 AM, parents need to be able to step in to prohibit fatigued driving.

Who Can Report Misconduct? Many model TDAs refer only to a ticket or citation issued by law enforcement, but what if a teacher, coach, neighbor, friend, relative, or even a fellow student tells the parent, "I saw your teen texting while driving," or "I saw several passengers in the car"? What if the parent receives an anonymous tip?

This is, I think, a parent's judgment call, which should be based on whether the report is from a credible source. The agreement should note that suspensions may result from reports or events other than official, police-issued tickets.

No Fault. To balance the parent override, the agreement should also state that driving privileges will not be suspended if your teen calls for a ride to avoid an unsafe situation or is involved in a crash where the teen driver is plainly not at fault. If the teen is stopped at a light and rear-ended, or his or her car is dented while parked, no consequence should occur.

Technology. If you, as a parent, can afford to install one of the evolving technologies for tracking teen drivers, write this into the agreement and make it clear that data from that device can result in a suspension. For example, if a device measuring the speed of the car sends the parent an e-mail report if a certain speed has been exceeded, a suspension should result.

Who Signs the Agreement? Obviously, the teen driver must sign, but the agreement should also be signed by every adult who will have some role in continued training and supervision of the teen's driving. Having all responsible adults sign may prevent the teen from trying to avoid a suspension by lobbying an adult who did not sign, and it serves the all-important purpose of making sure that all supervising adults agree with each other about what the rules will be.

Where? Keep one copy of the signed agreement in the car, and one with each person who signed it.

Already Licensed? Can a TDA be negotiated with a teen who is already licensed and driving? Absolutely. A violation or crash will provide an opening for a parent to insist on one as a condition of further driving, but the best advice is to not delay putting a TDA in place for every teen driver.

At the end of this book is my model TDA. This is a national model that needs to be adapted to your state's GDL laws and your household. It is downloadable in English or Spanish on the landing page of my blog, www.fromreidsdad.org. In this model I have tried to take the best features of existing teen driver contracts and improve upon them, to better reflect the current best practices that supervising adults should use with their teen drivers.

My model offers the following combination:

- a statement of purpose;
- a reminder that the agreement needs to be consistent with your state's law;
- a recommendation to introduce the agreement before your teen obtains a learner's permit and review it again when he or she gets a full license (that is, the right to drive solo);
- acknowledgments, initialed separately by the teen driver and each supervising adult, of each of the critical dangers of teen driving, including delayed brain development;
- a separate acknowledgment by supervising adults (to show teens that this agreement is a two-way street) of their positions as role models and teachers of safe driving habits;
- a reminder that adult supervision of teen driving is an ongoing, day-by-day, circumstance-by-circumstance task that requires judgment;
- a clear statement against joyriding, by requiring a driving plan;
- a specific teen driver promise to pull over and stop safely before texting, typing, reading, watching video, or making a call;
- recognition that misconduct reports can come to supervising adults from a variety of sources;
- clear times and procedures for curfews and use of any exceptions;
- a minimum time period (one year suggested) for the agreement;
- identification of any technology to be used;
- a statement of who will pay for what portion of the expenses;

- the option to use a neutral third party as a mediator; and
- most importantly, a *commitment* to safety and following the terms of the agreement.

Regarding the provision on "Finances": as a result of the economic downturn that began in 2008, parents have spent less in recent years on teen driving, and teens have had less to spend on driving. Driving is expensive. Insurance rates for teens have always been much higher than they are for older drivers (and with good reason, given teens' crash rates); the escalating price of gas has only made things worse. In difficult economic times, teen driving is something of a luxury. The lower teen crash rates of the past several years are due in part to stricter teen driver laws but also to troubles in our economy.

We can feel badly about all of this, but the cost of driving should lead us to consider one important way that parents can control their teen drivers—through purse strings. *Money is another way for parents to say no.* Whether by explaining the family budget to your teen and showing what would have to be cut if the family allocated more to nonessential gasoline, or refusing keys on a particular day because of a recent, unexpected expense, the financial costs of driving are a way to exert control—and a way that teens are hard-pressed to challenge. Using a family budget to control a teen driver might even have the beneficial effect of teaching about the fiscal realities of life—budgeting, prioritizing expenses, pinching pennies, and saving.

The cost of driving is a difficult challenge for millions of Americans, but parents, whatever the family's economic situation, should bear in mind that money is one important way to regulate teen driving, and the Finances line in a TDA is a place to start.

10

The Difference Between Purposeful Driving and Joyriding

I learned a critical lesson from the driving instructors who served with me on my state's task force. Their point was so obvious that I wasn't sure why it had not occurred to me while I was supervising my son's driving, but it hadn't. I suspect now that for most parents, this idea, this key caution, lies just beneath the surface of our consciousness: if John or Sue has a reason to drive from Point A to Point B, a prescribed route, an estimated time of arrival, and a consequence for not arriving on time, the likelihood of a serious crash is relatively low. But when teens drive for the sake of driving, without a particular destination, reason, planned route, or arrival time, trouble starts. If teens are driving for kicks, to get away from parents or something else at home, to spend time in a car with friends, or perhaps to see just what this four-wheeled contraption can do, crash rates are high.

Simply, I learned the difference between "purposeful" and "recreational" driving. Recreational driving is also known as joyriding.

If your teen is headed to sports practice or a job at 6:00 AM and arriving late will result in extra pushups, less playing time, or docked pay, he or she will drive the shortest, quickest route—and will most likely get there safely. If, however, the evening's agenda is a ride "somewhere," to a destination unknown, and with a return time that is merely "sometime before" a curfew, significant motivations for teens to drive safely disappear and factors that can cause a crash take their place. Teens are more likely to practice the safe driving skills they have learned and obey both teen driving and traffic safety laws when their destination is itself a goal. Conversely, when teens drive for entertainment or escape instead of transportation, the priority of safety takes a figurative back seat.

The difference between purposeful and recreational will not always be clear. If a teenage boy is driving cross-town to see his girlfriend and then go to the movies, is that purposeful (the driver has a reason, an estimated arrival time, and a consequence) or recreational? Even so, the vast majority of situations where teens get behind the wheel fall into one category or the other.

Parents are the first line of defense against teen drivers getting into situations where the risk of a crash is heightened. If the driving that your son or daughter proposes today, tonight, or tomorrow can be labeled cruising, joyriding, hanging, hauling, dragging, going for a spin, wheeling, tooling, tracking, scoping, surfing, or some current teen slang equivalent, then think twice about allowing your teen to take the keys and go.

Getting a Teen to Acknowledge the Risks

Teenagers often operate in their own private world, focusing on themselves and how they fit in with their peers. They regard themselves as immune or invulnerable to life's dangers.

Parents are asked to entrust car keys to these limited-vision beings.

So how do we get teen drivers to acknowledge and internalize the risks of driving, and to modify their behavior? Obviously, teens are capable of protecting themselves. They know not to step off a cliff, to jump into the path of an oncoming train, or to touch a high-voltage wire. How do we push driving into this category of clearly understood dangers?

In driver education (whether received from a commercial school or parents/guardians), and in materials provided by motor vehicle departments, police, schools, and advocacy groups, two approaches predominate: gruesome videos and photos, and getting teens to understand how bad driving decisions will impact their families, friends, and communities. Herewith, a strong vote for the second approach.

Not going out on a limb: I would observe that teens in our society are desensitized to blood, guts, gore, body parts, mangled cars, and crash scenes. Millions of people pay money to go to the movies just for the thrill of seeing exactly these things—high-speed car chases, crashes, explosions, and injury and death.

The most prominent recent example of the gruesome approach to safer teen driving is the "Gwent Police Department" video, produced in 2009 in Wales. The video shows the slow-motion death of several girls in a car whose driver was texting. This video, packed with heads snapping back, twisted metal, dislocated body parts, and blood, has been a worldwide hit on YouTube. It has been popular, I think, not because it graphically demonstrates the dangers of texting, but because it shows injuries and death in slow motion. Its effect is titillating, not cautionary. In my view, videos and photos of automobile crashes and injuries are not terribly effective in sensitizing our teens to the dangers of teen driving.

Contrast this approach with teens listening to searing personal testimony from parents and siblings of teen drivers who have lost their lives. This is the approach taken by !MPACT, or Mourning Parents Act, www.mourningparentsact.org. !MPACT was founded by mothers who lost their teens in crashes a few weeks apart in 2002. The leaders of !MPACT tell thousands of high school students each year about when their teen left the house, how they learned that their teen had been in a serious crash, and how they learned that their son or daughter had died. And then the details of the crash and injuries. And then their agonizing descent into shock, disbelief, and horror, as they realized that there would be no more birthdays, graduations, and weddings.

At !MPACT presentations, when these mothers, fathers, and siblings speak, you can hear a pin drop in the auditorium. These students are not texting or whispering. They are fully engaged in considering their own mortality. They are immersed in the message being delivered and what it would sound like if their own mother, father, sister, or brother were speaking. Tears flow, and invariably students send messages to the presenters about how their remarks have led to changes in their habits as drivers and passengers. Sometimes these teens confess in their messages to near crashes that almost cost them their lives. The lessons of !MPACT and similar organizations are:

- getting teens to internalize the dangers of driving is critical;
- too often, we try to convey lessons about safe driving with photos and videos that feature blood and twisted metal; and
- we would do better to focus more on the human consequences of bad driving decisions, on the multidimensional and incalculable suffering that follows serious injury or death of a teen driver.

So forget the bloody videos and ask your teen's school to invite an organization like !MPACT or a speaker who can deliver a compelling personal story to come and speak about the risks of teen driving. Or introduce your teen to someone in your community who is willing to be a real-life example. There are, unfortunately, quite a few of us to ask.

12

The Ceremony of the Keys

It is standard advice to parents of teen drivers: "You are the keeper of the keys." Let's explore what this means.

In general, of course, no keys, no car. If parents withhold keys, teens don't drive, and there are no teen driver crashes. But except for putting off driving to a more mature age, the question arises with teens of when, where, and how to take custody of and hand over car keys.

The starting point is to keep in mind the powerful if not exalted position of being a parent. A parent is the dragon that guards the treasure. No one gets by who shouldn't. Parents are the parole board that decides who gets released and when. They are the ones who decide whether an inexperienced and risk-prone person will be allowed to operate a piece of heavy machinery that has the potential to injure or kill others. We hold a position of responsibility to our families, and of trust to everyone else who will be on the same street or highway as our teen drivers.

What should a teen need to do to obtain the keys? First and foremost is *to have to ask for them*. Keys should not be readily available to any teen driver. They should not be just one more article in the bin on the kitchen counter. To go back to the air traffic controller analogy (chapter 8), the exercise of a teen asking for the keys each time he or she wants to get behind the wheel is a parent's opportunity to review the flight plan, to conduct a safety check: Weather suitable for an inexperienced driver? Destination and time of arrival and departure established? Route mapped out? Driver rested, alert, and not overly stressed? The teen's trip should be purposeful, not recreational (chapter 10). The main points of the teen-parent agreement (chapter 9) should be briefly reviewed. *Handing over the keys should be a ceremony that highlights the seriousness of the activity at hand.*

Where does a parent keep the keys? Hiding them is one option, although if my experience with my son is any guide, this may be a doubtful strategy. Concealing the keys only sets off a game of hide-and-seek. The hiding seemed to underscore a lack of trust and undermine the also-important message that driving is a very adult action. (Also, on one occasion, I forgot where I had hidden the keys.) On the other hand, it is hard to advocate that the keys be available in plain sight of your teen, governed only by an understanding—even if stated in the teen driver agreement—that she will ask for the keys each time before driving. There should be a middle ground. I advocate having the keys available on a stand-alone hook, in plain sight of supervising parents, so everyone knows when the keys are there and when they have been taken. Perhaps the Tips from Reid's Dad list at the end of this book (chapter 26) will be taped to the wall next to the key hook. In this way, their location is not secret, but taking them will be a deliberate, contemplative, public step. Doing this, I think, emphasizes that the keys are being made available in return for a renewed safety review and pledge.

Whether handing over the keys is tied to other matters such as completion of homework and chores is your business, but my own view is that driving is driving and, like a driving contract, should be separate from other parent-teen matters. We have enough to think about with teen driving without mixing in other parts of life.

Being the custodian of keys is a somewhat different undertaking when your teen is the primary driver of the car, as opposed to one of several drivers of a family car or cars. Research has demonstrated that teens who have their own cars have higher crash rates than those who rely on a parent's or sibling's car (chapter 17). This advice about keys, therefore, is doubly important if your teen has his or her own car.

Car keys are a parent's leverage. Use it. Make each time your teen gets behind the wheel an investiture ceremony, a conferring of knighthood. Keep firmly in mind what is at stake and what is at risk when a teen becomes the Keeper of the Keys.

13

The Unappreciated Danger of Passengers, Even Siblings

One of the saddest realities of media coverage of teen driver crashes is headlines and articles that describe one or more passengers being injured or killed. Crashes like my son's, where the teen driver was killed but the passengers survived, are often the exception.

A 2012 study by the AAA Foundation reviewed nearly ten thousand crashes from 2005 to 2010 in which a sixteen- or seventeen-year-old driver died while transporting one or more passengers. The study documents that while overall crash rates for teens declined during the analysis period, the crash rate for young drivers with passengers was essentially unchanged—which indicates that even as teen driving laws have gotten stricter across the nation, an unchanging percentage of parents and teens have continued to ignore them. In fact, the study shows that teen drivers with teen passengers is becoming the most intractable problem in teen driving.

The study's second chilling statistic is that among those nearly ten thousand driver fatalities, nearly two thirds were boys.

As noted earlier, teen driver laws vary by state, and passenger restrictions are among the most variable. This reality, combined with the evidence compiled by AAA and the fact that parents are in the best position to supervise a teen driver's passengers, means that enforcement of passenger restrictions offers the greatest potential for reduction of current crash levels; the more lenient a state's passenger rules, the more vigilant a parent must be; and roughly speaking, boys need more supervision than girls.

The fact that driving is the leading cause of death of people under twenty in the United States leads to this question: At what age do kids begin to be at risk as passengers? National statistics provide the answer: age twelve. Junior high school. Another question is: During what time of day are teen passengers most at risk? Here too the answer is clear from the data: the hours directly after school, when kids are most likely to pile into cars without parents present to say, "Not so fast," and with freedom and fun most on their minds.

Advice about passengers is best broken into four categories: risks, myths, advice for parents of driver and passengers, and tips for schools and youth organizations.

Risks: Parents who conclude that it is safe for their child to ride with a teen driver because that driver is a sensible kid who has taken driver's ed are playing with fire. The best advice about riding with a teen driver is *don't*.

But since this may happen, the fallback is to identify the factors that increase the baseline dangers of teen driving: recreational driving (driving without a destination, a prescribed route, a timetable, and a consequence for arriving late); distracted driving (texting or using an electronic device); doing anything that takes eyes off the road, hands off the wheel, or mind off the situation; impaired driving (drugs, alcohol, fatigue); driving at night, or in bad weather; driving in an unfamiliar place; and driving without a seat belt. At least avoid these higher-risk situations.

Myths: An adult driver who is specifically supervising a teen driver, and is sitting in the front passenger seat, can be regarded as a second pair of eyes. However, to think that having another teen, an inexperienced driver, or anyone in the back seat improves safety by being an additional pair of eyes is simply inaccurate. The potential for distraction outweighs the additional vigilance.

Some parents justify allowing teen drivers to have illegal passengers because it saves on gas. I wonder how many times a teen passenger actually pays for a share of gas, but in any event, the cost of gasoline is trivial compared to the documented dangers—and the personal and financial cost—of teen drivers having passengers. The same is true of the explanation that a teen driver needs passengers to get experience driving with passengers. Teens should learn to become safe drivers first; then they can move on to learning to drive safely with passengers.

Parent rules: Passengers are a topic for which it is simple for parents to set down clear rules: No passengers that are illegal under state law. No passengers without the express permission of the parent/ supervising adult of the teen driver and the passenger. No exceptions, and this should be clear in the teen driving agreement that you and your teen negotiate and sign.

If your child must ride with a teen, don't allow him or her to get in a car with a teen driver who is not known to you—as best you can determine—to be a responsible person, an experienced driver (at least one year with a full license and no suspensions or crashes) who legally may carry passengers. Only purposeful driving should be allowed; joyrides should be prohibited. Communicate with the driver's parent or supervising adult so everyone is aware of the plan. Explain to your teen clearly not to tolerate any form of distraction or impairment by the teen driver. Rehearse a strategy for how your teen, as a passenger, will get out of the car if the situation becomes unsafe (the most popular is "I feel like I am going to throw up"). Have a code word that your teen can text or say in a cell phone call if he or she is in danger. Make it clear that the decision to get out of the car of a distracted, impaired, or unsafe driver, even in the middle of nowhere, can be the difference between life and death. And don't forget that pets can be dangerous distractions.

For schools and youth organizations: Every school or organization that relies in any way on teens transporting other students should make sure that all permission forms have a clear statement of that state's law regarding passengers. Chapter 20 provides a suggestion for using a portion of a school's website to post a list of the teen drivers who have had their license long enough to legally carry passengers.

Although the passenger restrictions of many GDL laws allow teens to transport their sisters and brothers earlier than other passengers, research shows that the distraction risk is equally great. Our age-of-licensing laws, unfortunately, are based more on tradition than science or traffic safety facts. Study after study during the past decade has documented that crash rates of newly licensed teen drivers increase significantly when they have one or more passengers other than a supervising adult driver. Allowing siblings as passengers of newly licensed teen drivers is guaranteed to increase crash rates and put both teen drivers and their siblings at risk. If laws were based on current research and statistics, siblings would not be allowed as passengers earlier than others.

Driving instructors that I have asked about this have explained that new drivers are still in learning mode and should not be distracted by siblings while they are learning. Learning to drive with the distractions of passengers is a skill for later in a driver's development. The safety concern is indisputable and should be decisive. As traffic researcher Dave Preusser has observed, "Would you trust your most precious cargo to your most inexperienced driver?"

Siblings as passengers are as distracting as nonsiblings, and in some situations more so.

14

Managing Curfews

Teen driver laws in most states set nighttime restrictions, most importantly a curfew. In general, the deadline for teen drivers to be off the road ranges from 9:00 PM to midnight, with several exceptions, such as employment, school activities, medical needs, religious observances, and participation in volunteer public safety services (fire, ambulance, "safe rides," and the like), each of which can necessitate later driving.

Here are some thoughts on curfews and how to manage them:

- Curfews do not address the dangerous one or two hours after school. It is at those times that teens are most likely to be riding with illegal passengers, which substantially increases crash rates. Curfews only target late-night driving.

- As to late-night driving, a constant problem is teen drivers racing home to beat the curfew. In fact, some teens think that getting off the road by the state's deadline is a legitimate reason to drive at whatever speed is necessary to get home on time.

- Curfews do not justify speeding, of course, but they do highlight the importance of planning to ensure that teens will be off the road without speeding. Doing so requires a discussion, before the teen leaves, about the route and the anticipated return trip travel time. Once these are established, parent and teen are better able to plan to comply with the curfew. The departure should also build in a margin for traffic delay; if the route normally takes thirty minutes and the curfew is 11:00 PM, then departure time should be 10:15 PM.

- The teen driver should understand that a delay such as a traffic backup that will result in missing the curfew needs to be reported to a parent or guardian as soon as it can be done safely; that is, not by texting or using a cell phone while driving, but by getting to a safe, off-road location at the earliest opportunity to explain the location and extent of the delay. The teen should understand that delays first reported upon arrival at home will be thoroughly questioned.

- School events and activities that end after 9:00 PM are a significant problem, because they result in teens driving during the most dangerous hours of the day, often with passengers and when fatigue is likely, so supervising adults should realize that they may need to be chauffeurs even to newly licensed drivers to avoid this dangerous situation.

- If the parent and teen have executed a teen driving agreement, they have most likely identified a penalty for missing a curfew. This provision requires a parent's judgment. As we all know, predicting driving time is an inexact science, and there will be times when teens will arrive late due to conditions beyond their control. Recall that the purpose of a TDA is a mutual commitment to safety, not a punishment for the slightest infraction. If the teen was diligent in leaving on time, provides a credible explanation for being a few minutes late, and is not a repeat offender, flexibility is appropriate.

- As for managing the exceptions to curfews stated in your state's law, the first, simple rule is: if the teen will be on the road after the state's curfew on a regular basis, most likely for employment or a school activity, have the employer or a school official provide a letter, on letterhead, that the teen can keep in the glove box. The letter should specify when the teen will be on the road, why, and the route. An employer's letter might say: "To Whom It May Concern/Law Enforcement: Kevin Jones is an employee of the 7-11 Store on Midland Avenue in Smithtown. He works until midnight on Friday, Saturday, and Sunday, after which he drives to his home at 123 Main Street, using Route 14." A school official's might say: "Mary Doe is involved in a theater production at Central High School from April 16 to May 4. She will leave school Monday through Thursday night between 11:00 PM and midnight and drive to her home at 18 Elm Street, using the River Parkway."

- Teens need to understand the limits on using exceptions. When I speak to high school students, I tell them: "If the curfew is 11:00 PM and it's 11:15 PM because the game went into overtime, and the police stop you, but you are somewhere close to a direct line between school and your home, you're not breaking the law. But if it's 2:00 AM and you're two towns away, you're in trouble."

- Parents should bear in mind that a joyride with a curfew is still a joyride and therefore dangerous. The fact that a teen may be ordered home from joyriding driving (see chapter 10) by a certain time does not lessen the huge dangers of the joyride itself.

- Finally, recognize that the nighttime curfew in a state's teen driver law is a *minimum*. Use your judgment on a case-by-case basis. Exercise your rights under your TDA. Err on the side of earlier than state law (such as 9:00 PM for new drivers) and allow exceptions when justified. If particular circumstances such as fatigue or bad weather counsel you to set an earlier curfew for a particular evening, by all means do so. As with all other parts of teen driver laws, the state sets one curfew for all teens in all circumstances. This does not mean that you, as a parent, park your judgment in the garage.

15

Supervising the Brand-New Driver

Although parents would like to believe that training teen drivers is a linear equation, that teens become better drivers as they log more hours behind the wheel, it is well documented that *driving deteriorates when teens begin to drive unsupervised*—not because skills deteriorate but because attitudes change. During the first six months that teens drive solo, with no one there to monitor or correct them, they are prone to experiment and jettison whatever parts of instruction they think are stupid. In particular, brand-new drivers take aim at parent hypocrisy, adopting the bad driving habits that parents or guardians warned them about because the parents regularly made these mistakes as well. In fact, this phenomenon most highlights the facts that parents are role models for young drivers, and at no time is a parent's own driving more consequential than when a teen has a learner's permit and is scrutinizing every parent or guardian driving habit. If parents use distracting electronics, don't buckle up, speed, tailgate, don't signal, or drive impaired, they should *expect* their teens to copy them when they begin driving by themselves.

So, just when parents may think that their teens are doing fine—no crash yet—they should be more vigilant than ever, because some of their training evaporates when teens drive unsupervised.

There is no magic answer to this dilemma, but three approaches may help. The first is to provide your teen far more on-the-road training hours than state law requires. Perhaps if the teen has hundreds of hours at the wheel instead of the twenty to fifty that most states require, he or she will have more ingrained good habits. The next is for parents to realize that a teen beginning to drive unsupervised is not the end of supervised training. Parents can ease their teens slowly into this stage, alternating supervised and unsupervised driving for the first several months.

A third way, if affordable, is to install one of the teen driver tracking technologies; those that report on the car's speed and location and can even set geographic boundaries for the teen driver's vehicle are the most important at the start. Teens whose unsupervised driving is electronically monitored will be, by definition and in result, more accountable. (Businesses with large fleets of vehicles have long used technology to keep track of where their vehicles are, and more recently, to monitor the conduct of their drivers. These systems have now been adapted to allow parents to track their teen's driving, and a variety of products are available to parents, some at modest cost.)

Obviously, these systems continue to evolve and improve, such that any detailed description of capabilities could be outdated in a matter of months. Suffice it to say that, basically, these systems electronically track vehicle location and speed and transmit a report to supervising adults. Some systems use boxes that rest on the dashboard (which can give sneaky teens a way to evade them), while others are hardwired into the vehicle. Some track and report in "real time" (every few minutes) while others generate periodic (such as monthly) reports. A few systems, not unlike electric fences for pets, set geographic boundaries and give the teen a warning signal and supervising adults a report if the vehicle breaches the set boundaries.

Another consideration for parents is that some insurance companies will consider a discount on premiums for teen drivers if tracking technology will be used. If parents can afford them, these systems are a useful tool for managing teen drivers. A teen's knowledge that his/her driving conduct is being electronically monitored can only help. Moreover, any teen who tries to disable or outsmart a tracking system will surely raise a red flag about not being ready to take safe driving seriously.

So, with the caveat that these systems are in no way a basis for parents to otherwise let their guard down, tracking technology, if affordable, is a sensible proactive step.

16

Traffic Tickets as a Teaching Moment

Picture this: your teen, a licensed driver for several months, receives a ticket from a police officer for violating some provision of your state's teen driver laws—speeding, carrying illegal passengers, driving after curfew, violating cell phone restrictions, committing a moving violation. The teen pleads with you that she didn't do it, or the police made a mistake, or the officer singled her out from among other drivers whose driving was much worse because she's a teenager. Or the police were sneaky, lying in wait behind a sign or a tree. "It's just not fair!" pleads your young driver. This was her first direct encounter with the police.

A teen driver receiving a ticket sets three things in motion for parents/guardians and teens. First, the parent and teen need to talk through what happened (and get past the initial denials). Second, the teen driver and parent need to decide whether they will challenge the ticket or accept the consequences—paying a fine, incurring driving record points, or receiving a license suspension. Third, parent and teen need to decide *when* they are going to respond.

This third decision is important. It is influenced by the fact that there is almost always an administrative lag time between when police issue a ticket and when the government processes the driver's response or a court issues a hearing date.

Every state administers tickets differently for driving violations. Weeks or even months can elapse between when a ticket is issued to a teen driver and when she receives notice of the penalty for a violation or notice of a court date. Meanwhile, unless the parent and teen have signed a teen driving agreement that results in an immediate suspension, or the parent imposes an on-the-spot suspension, the teen may continue to drive.

For the parent of a teen driver, this situation and these decisions (what happened, how to respond, and when) are a critical teaching moment. At stake are your teen's respect for the law in general, teen driver laws in particular, and law enforcement; and his understanding that driving implicates the safety of dozens of other people. Your approach to each of these issues will affect your teen's approach to driving.

This concern about parent conduct and guidance is not hypothetical. In 2007, Massachusetts adopted a mandatory license suspension system for teens who violated its GDL laws. Suspensions started at sixty days for a first offense and went up from there for repeat offenses. Within months of the start of enforcement, the news media began to report about parents resisting fiercely—screaming at prosecutors and court personnel, doing everything possible to avoid suspensions of their teen's licenses. These parents were no doubt angry about the inconvenience of once again having to again drive their teens to school and events and losing their new in-house pickup and delivery service. But what struck me about these news articles was envisioning the teens standing there, watching their parents challenge and disparage police, prosecutors, court staff, and even judges.

I recognize that police can make mistakes, and that sometimes they use enforcement techniques such as speed traps that can seem unfair. Police can appear arbitrary when ticketing some while letting other offenders go unpunished. Moreover, a police officer stopping a teen driver can create the perception that the teen has been profiled, that is, stopped due to her apparent age rather than her driving.

But back to the teaching moment and the three issues: while parents should review with their teens the events that led to the ticket, they should also recognize that factually baseless tickets are a relatively rare occurrence. One of the best assurances we have that tickets issued to teen drivers usually have some actual basis is that the police generally have far more responsibilities than they can handle; they issue tickets when misconduct genuinely threatens public safety.

If we assume that most tickets have some basis, then we can focus on the key point: a parent's reaction and approach to a teen driver's ticket presents a critical opportunity to reinforce several safe driving lessons. Parents, please:

- don't disparage the teen driving laws or law enforcement;

- push back against your teen's insistence that the police officer was mistaken, arbitrary, vindictive, or stupid;

- direct your teen to accept the consequence of her action;

- don't argue with prosecutors or court staff about your teen's conduct;

- don't let inconvenience or cost to you get in the way of these lessons; and

- *don't delay*; have your teen take the medicine. Don't ask a court for repeated continuances (delays), and don't make excuses ("She has a quiz/game/lesson") that pale in comparison to safety.

Another, somewhat hidden side of the situation after law enforcement issues a ticket, is the time it can take from when the ticket is issued to when it is enforced through a fine or license suspension by a Motor Vehicle Department or the court system. Most states and some big cities have a central processing bureau, so that when the police issue a ticket, the ticket is sent to that bureau, which sends a notice of the violation to the teen driver's home. (Whether parents of teen drivers who receive tickets should be notified at the same time is an interesting policy or administrative issue; most states do not do so.) If the punishment is only a monetary fine, the teen either pays the fine and that is the end of it, or goes to court to contest the fine, which may result in a reduction or a deal with a prosecutor. In some states, paying the fine is an admission of wrongdoing that results in an automatic license suspension. If the penalty is license suspension, the driver either accepts the suspension, sends in the acknowledgment, has the license suspended, and then endures the no-license period, or the driver goes to court, seeking to have the suspension modified or reversed. Finally, in some states, a ticket or a repeat violation triggers a mandatory driver retraining, where the teen driver reports to the motor vehicle department or a driving school for a refresher.

But the question is: What should a parent do with a teen driver *while* the police, the motor vehicle department, the processing agency, and the court system sort all of this out? First, this situation illustrates one key benefit of a teen driving agreement. If a parent and teen have negotiated and signed one, it provides the first answer, an immediate suspension of driving for some period of time as agreed to in the agreement, regardless of whether or when the government acts. (In my model agreement, this immediate suspension is in addition to whatever government imposes, so that misconduct has two penalties.)

Second is to realize that the issuance of a ticket should be a loud alarm that a teen is at risk, especially if the violation involved something like speeding, carrying illegal passengers, not wearing a seat belt, consuming alcohol or drugs, or similar serious offenses. In other words, don't let the fact that the government takes time to impose a punishment lull you as a parent into taking the violation as anything less than a serious development requiring your own immediate discipline and increased oversight.

The administrative delay that can follow a teen getting a ticket or citation should not cause parents to let their guard down. If anything, it should go way, way up.

17

Car Buying and Sharing, and Saving on Gas

While the title of this chapter could suggest that choosing a particular make and model car somehow overcomes the risks discussed in previous chapters, this is not the case. The only advice for this topic that is consistent with this book is: *the best car for a teen may well be no car.* I concede, however, that much of this book is also about bowing to but then proactively managing reality, so let me present the accumulated wisdom on this topic.

The best practices here are not rocket science. Cars with the most safety features are the best. The characteristics to consider for a teen driver's car are:

- air bags (driver, front passenger, side, curtain);
- crash ratings;
- electronic stability control and antilock brakes (standard on 2012 models);
- horsepower (over 300 is considered "high performance," and dangerous for an inexperienced driver);

- vehicle weight to horsepower ratio (which some experts say should be less than 15:1);

- rollover ratings (SUVs and pickup trucks have higher centers of gravity, making them more susceptible to rollovers);

- acceleration (zero to sixty in not less than eight or more than eleven seconds);

- braking distance;

- visibility on all sides from the driver's seat;

- rear bumper camera;

- steel reinforced doors; and

- impact-absorbing designs and materials.

Automobile technology is evolving, and manufacturers are introducing new safety features each year; automatic stopping sensors, and maximum speed governors are just a few. Experts and drivers need to evaluate these new gadgets to see if they improve safety and are cost-effective. In the meantime, if you are considering buying a new or used car for a teen, or allowing a teen to buy one, the best advice is to postpone, and the second-best is to be sure the vehicle includes as many of the safety features listed above as possible.

Parents and teens also should not neglect old-fashioned provisioning of a vehicle with equipment and tools (in addition to tire-changing) for emergencies and bad weather: extra motor oil and windshield fluid, battery cables, a small fire extinguisher, a tire pressure gauge, a flashlight, a pen and pad, ice-scraper/brush, shovel, and duct tape.

As to buying a car for a teen driver, Children's Hospital of Philadelphia (CHOP) has made safe teen driving research and education a priority and publishes a superb website about teen driving, found at www.teendriversource.org. One CHOP study provides statistical evidence regarding this critical caution for parents of teen drivers: *teens who are permitted to have their own cars or to be the primary drivers of a particular car have higher crash rates than those who share a car with a parent or another family member.*

In a 2009 publication, CHOP recited these statistics (which, given everything that is in this book, should be regarded as frightening):

- Almost three of every four teen drivers in the United States have "primary access" to a vehicle (which I assume means they can drive the car whenever they want, so long as they can obtain the keys and permission; that is, they do not have to wait for someone else to finish using the vehicle).

- Teens with primary access to a car drive about 6.6 hours and 200 miles per week, as compared to 130 miles in 4.3 hours for those who share a car.

- Crash rates for teens with primary access are more than double those who rely on a shared car.

The hospital's study admirably compiles and presents the statistical case against giving teens primary access, but it seems to me that the reasons for this marked difference go beyond what can be demonstrated statistically. If a teen shares a car with a parent, the following good things are likely to happen: the parent keeps a closer watch on whether and when the teen gets behind the wheel in the first place; the parent is more likely to be attuned to the difference between purposeful and recreational driving; the teen is more likely to have to requisition the keys from the parent; the parent is more likely to make an informed, day-by-day, case-by-case judgment on whether it is safe for the teen to drive; the parent and teen are more likely, before the teen leaves, to put together at least an informal plan for the driving route, passengers, arrival time, check-in time, and return time; and the parent and teen are more likely to consider, at least momentarily, whether the teen driving at that particular moment is allowed under the teen driving agreement that they hopefully have signed.

At a basic parent-teen level, it seems that what is going on here is that when a teen shares a car with a parent, the parent is more motivated to be proactive, if only to protect the value of the car and the parent's own convenience, than a parent whose teen has his or her own car. Conversely, teens just don't want to face the consequences of crashing Mom's or Dad's car.

CHOP's study is simple, clear, and in line with common sense: buying your teen his or her own car, or giving your teen primary access to a car, substantially increases the risk of a crash, injury, or fatality. By contrast, forcing a teen to share a car reinforces good parenting and oversight across the board.

And then there is the price of gasoline. This is a push and pull, a double-edged sword, for teen driver safety.

Teen driver crash rates have been declining modestly but steadily during the past several years. Undoubtedly, stricter Graduated Driver Licensing laws and more attentive parents are contributing factors, but more expensive gasoline and the economic recession also have been influences. Obviously, as driving becomes more expensive, all drivers and especially teens and people whose income has declined drive fewer miles. By definition, this translates into fewer crashes and fatalities. Moreover, in these difficult economic times, where jobs for teens are scarce, teens are separated from a key source of gas money. Fewer jobs for teens and less income mean less driving and fewer crashes and injuries.

The high cost of refueling also has the beneficial effect of limiting teens to purposeful driving and reducing joyriding. Parents are clamping down out of economic necessity, not just safety, on their teens taking the car to hang out with friends. In this way, more expensive gas directly reduces a mode of teen driving—without a purpose, route, timetable, and consequence for arriving late—that is among the most dangerous for teens.

On the other hand, there are safety downsides to more expensive gas. The first is that teens get less practice behind the wheel; instruction itself has become more financially burdensome. Another negative is that parents are economically motivated to bend or violate state driving laws. Passenger restrictions have a cost: expensive gas gives parents a reason to combine driving practice with times when siblings and other illegal passengers are in the car, even if this practice is against the law. Paradoxically then, gas prices get in the way of the precious hours of practice that teen driver laws promote, and this can lead parents to set a bad example by allowing teens to drive in illegal situations.

A third significant result of the cost of gas for teen drivers is the incentive to share the pump price with passengers. As the literature and research on teen driving clearly establish, teen driver crash rates go up substantially with each additional passenger who is not an instructor or supervisor. On the other hand, $4.00 per gallon and higher gas prices, especially for teens driving every day to school, a job, or community service or events, are a compelling reason to divide the expense with passengers, even if they are illegal and unsafe.

High gas prices require every family to make hard choices about important matters—as basic as where we live in relation to jobs, schools, services, and stores. Yet as difficult as these decisions can be, for parents of teen drivers who put safety ahead of cost, the choices are clear:

- use gas prices to help your teens learn the reality that driving can be financially expensive;

- take the reduction in teen driving that results from high gas prices as a net gain for safety;

- don't give in to the temptation or incentive to use high gas prices as an excuse to violate teen driver laws;

- accept that high gas prices give parents another good reason to say no to teens who want to go for a joyride; and

- understand that when calculating the costs of gas against the costs of injury or even loss of life, there is simply no comparison.

18

Distracted Driving: Texting, "Connected Cars," GPS, and Headphones

Distracted driving resulting from use of electronic devices has caught the nation's attention. The federal government, traffic safety advocates, schools, insurance companies, and even personal injury lawyers have identified it as a growing danger.

Distracted driving differs from impaired driving. Distractions are activities or devices that divert an otherwise alert driver's attention. Impairments (generally, alcohol, drugs, and fatigue) continuously impact a driver's physical and mental ability to operate a vehicle and respond to traffic conditions, even while the driver is trying to pay full attention.

Parents of teen drivers need to know three things about distracted driving: what it is, why it is so dangerous, and what rules they should set and try to enforce with their teens.

A common definition of distracted driving is: hands off the wheel, eyes off the road, or mind off the driving situation. The first two are easy to understand: reaching into the back seat or trying to read a map while driving are common distractions. The third is more subtle. Scientists have now documented that when drivers—all drivers, of any age—are engaged in a conversation while driving, up to one-third of their brain function is diverted from evaluating the traffic situation ahead. In other words, talking while driving, even to a passenger, detracts to some degree from attention to the road. Conversations about emotional or heated topics are, of course, the most distracting. The technical term for driving with eyes open and hands on the wheel but with diminished attention to road conditions is "cognitive blindness."

The primary danger of distracted driving is that it diminishes or eliminates the driver's reaction time necessary to avoid a crash. At 30 mph, a car travels 143 feet in three seconds. At 60 mph, it's 286 feet, almost a football field. Avoiding a crash requires three steps: (1) comprehending the danger; (2) executing a maneuver to evade the danger; and (3) either slowing down or stopping the vehicle. In many instances, for an alert, responsive driver, each of the first two steps can take about one second. The third depends on speed, vehicle weight, and road conditions but usually requires several seconds. Thus, if a driver is distracted for even three seconds, his car traveling 60 mph covers a football field with no opportunity for the driver to take even the first step in avoiding a crash.

It is impossible to emphasize sufficiently how important it is for parents to warn and train their teens about the dangers of distracted driving. *Distraction and inattention, as much as speed or alcohol or passengers, are primary causes of teen driver crashes.* According to a recent NHTSA study, many teens do not even comprehend the danger, as nearly 30 percent surveyed did not regard taking their eyes off the road for up to ten seconds as an unsafe behavior. Teen drivers need every visual, manual, and cognitive ability and every bit of time available to help them discern the traffic situation and to respond appropriately. Thus, "no electronic device of any kind at any time" must be the rule for teens, no exceptions. Put another way: no use of an electronic device to text, type, read, watch video, or make a phone call when the car is not in park.

Three caveats go along with this ironclad rule as applied to electronic devices. The first is that there are ways for parents to check on whether their teens are using an electronic device, especially a cell phone, while driving. One of the realities of technology today is that it leaves a cyber footprint. Supervising adults should not hesitate to go online with their service provider, perform a post-driving review of the phone itself, or at least review monthly statements to check on a teen driver's cell phone use.

Second, parents should understand that state motor vehicle laws about use of electronic devices (for both teens and adult drivers) are a patchwork nationally, and often difficult to follow. For example, many state laws ban the use of cell phones but allow the use of "audio equipment" while driving. So may a teen driver use an iPod—audio equipment—while driving? The point is that, in this area in particular, parents *should ignore state law and its definitions and exemptions, and simply impose a "no device/no use" rule.*

A third caution is that teen drivers should use an electronic device only when they have stopped the car. "Stopped" means that the car is in "Park." A car in gear but stopped by a foot on the brake is still a vehicle capable of moving, and thus a risk.

It is essentially pointless to talk here about particular devices, such as apps that disable cell phones and texting while a vehicle is in motion. To write about today's technologies is to be outdated just months from now; indeed, one of the follies of state legislatures passing laws that purport to restrict or ban particular gadgets in cars is that these laws quickly become outdated. It's silly to parse through the ever-changing particulars of in-vehicle devices; all I can do is heighten parents' consciousness of the added risks of the various and evolving electronics.

Apps that disable cell phones or texting while driving are, I suppose, helpful in that they delay risky conduct, but we should not trust a technology whose purpose is to undo other technology. Installing technology and apps that disable the use of cell phones and texting when a car is in motion are the equivalent of placing a bomb inside the car—but then giving the driver a tool to defuse it. These apps make the double assumption that teens will drive *and* text, and the solution is to give them an additional piece of technology to counteract the danger that the first technology creates. *Parents should consider whether a teen who is likely to text while driving should ever get behind the wheel.* Unrealistic? Maybe, but my point is that in-vehicle technologies that try to counteract potentially deadly behavior are missing a critical point: our first priority must be to separate our new drivers from the inherent dangers; accepting them and then trying to mitigate them is the next level but should not be the starting point.

In any event: "texting" is the act of typing or reading a screen while driving. Never mind the device being typed on, or whether the typing is interactive use of the Internet or sending a message to a person. Whether the letters or numbers pushed are on a handheld mobile phone, a dashboard-mounted screen, or a laptop computer doesn't matter. Dialing a cell phone while driving is a form of texting. Reading letters or characters on a screen is also part of texting.

Texting is the most dangerous form of distracted driving because it involves all three of the highest-risk behaviors: the texter takes his eyes off the road, at least one hand off the wheel, and his mind off the driving situation.

Traffic safety researchers at Virginia Tech have calculated that a driver (again, of any age) who texts—types or reads—while driving is twenty-three times more likely to crash. The primary reason is that *the average act of sending a text message takes about five seconds, and thus completely eliminates the three-second minimum reaction time needed to avoid a crash, and more.*

Volumes have been written about texting. State and federal lawmakers have struggled to define it, but it's really very simple: no one should ever type on a keyboard or read a message on a screen while driving. Period.

While distracted driving is often characterized as a teen and young driver phenomenon arising from texting, new distracting technologies are moving into the adult driver mainstream. Auto manufacturers are adding distracting electronics, mainly as dashboard-mounted, multipurpose, interactive computer screens that offer not only telecommunications, navigation, and sound systems but also consumer electronics, video entertainment, and interactive Internet connections that allow use of social media. *Consumer Reports* has labeled vehicles equipped with interactive technology "connected cars." One auto manufacturer has described its goal as "iPhones with wheels." The functions, sophistication, and availability of these systems are limited only by the imaginations and collaborations of electronics and auto industry engineers and consumer preferences and budgets, but there does not appear to be any doubt that: dashboards will be the location, big screens will be the basic installation, distracting interactive functions will be the norm, and entirely preventable crashes and fatalities will be the result.

Predicting the exact shape of these imminent amenities is not my focus. The point is that while research is pouring in about the dangers of distracted driving, electronics and auto manufacturing companies are working as quickly as they can to introduce new features into cars that, we can predict with certainty, will compromise safety.

It appears that the universal defense from manufacturers is that they are only responding to consumer demand, and safety "is a matter of individual responsibility." In other words, if your car comes with a dashboard-mounted screen that allows you, while driving on an interstate, to launch a browser, search for the nearest restaurant, and display reviews of its food and service, then it is simply up to you as a driver to do so responsibly and safely.

The fallacy of this argument, of course, is that driving, more than any other activity in our society, implicates the safety of others. In no other activity does one person randomly threaten more people than when a driver takes his eyes off the road to interact with a video screen or use a keyboard.

Thus, we have ongoing today, simultaneously, not only nationwide efforts to improve safety but also to introduce into cars new technologies that will cause death and serious injury in exactly the ways that so many are trying to prevent. Distractions from electronic devices are fast becoming not just a young driver problem but also an adult driver phenomenon. Parents of teen drivers should keep in mind the implications of this trend: *parents are role models, and those who surf the Internet with their eyes and fingers while driving will have a harder time warning their teens about the dangers of texting.*

Which leads us to the most problematic device for teen drivers, the Global Positioning System, or GPS. The owner of a driving school once called me, saying that a parent of one of his teen driver students insisted that even though state law bans teen drivers from using any "mobile electronic device," GPS systems are exempt from such bans, or should be. He asked for help in responding.

This seemingly straightforward question turned out to be rather complex. I guess I should have figured out that the question was not easy from the fact that my first two reactions—perhaps yours also—were contradictory. On the one hand, a GPS helps us with directions, and so it is a safety aid. What could be wrong with that? On the other hand, a GPS is an electronic device with a screen and a keyboard, and thus exactly the kind of distraction from driving that causes crashes. These can't both be correct, I thought.

Many teen driver state laws prohibit the use of any "mobile electronic device" while driving. These laws often, also, refer to "any handheld or other portable electronic equipment," thereby including any texting device, pager, personal digital assistant, laptop computer, or video game. However, these definitions sometimes exclude equipment "installed for the purpose of providing navigation."

A GPS "provides navigation," right? But use of distracting electronic devices is strictly prohibited. So, if a teen driver takes her eye off the road to type in an address on a GPS, is she violating the law?

It appears that at least some state laws do not consider a GPS to be the type of electronic device that teen drivers should be prohibited from using. But let us as parents and instructors of teen drivers consider whether using a GPS is a good idea, legal or not.

GPS units are amazing devices that provide directions to our destination and pinpoint the location of our vehicle. The safety advantage can be substantial to drivers, emergency responders, and law enforcement. Yet consider these drawbacks:

- Unless the GPS is voice activated (and some are, but in my understanding, very few at this time), using one requires typing in an address, which is no different from, and every bit as dangerous as, texting if it occurs while the car is in motion.

- A GPS has a screen, which is unquestionably a distraction from the road ahead.

- A GPS is not infallible, of course, and perhaps the only thing more dangerous than a teen driver is a confused or lost teen driver.

- GPS voice commands, in a subtle way, direct us where and when to turn but may give the impression that it is safe to turn, which may or may not be the case. In other words, I worry that for a teen driver, a voice command from a GPS may be taken (as illogical as it may sound) as the GPS's evaluation that the turn can be made safely, as if the GPS has also evaluated traffic surrounding the vehicle.

- The simple fact is that teen drivers are still learning to drive, and a GPS is one more thing to think about.

All of the above considered, here are several recommendations for parents considering whether their teen driver should use a GPS:

- In general, for the reasons listed above, teen drivers should avoid using a GPS, if possible, even if it is technically legal.

- Don't let a GPS lull you or your teen into skipping one of the most important steps that should precede every time a teen driver gets behind the wheel—planning the intended route. Put another way, do not under any circumstances think that using a GPS is a reason to allow your teen to jump into a car and drive to an unfamiliar place without planning, because the GPS voice will show the way.

- If your teen intends to use a GPS, make its use a part of the teen's supervised training. Don't start a teen on a GPS for the first time when he or she begins to drive unsupervised.

- Emphasize to your teen that, if a GPS will/must be used, typing an address must be done before the car is in motion, and if the address needs to be revised, the teen should pull off the road into a safe place.

We should not even be debating whether teen drivers should use a GPS. It is surprising that teen driver laws don't ban GPS units as mobile electronic devices, and our anti-texting laws (for everyone else) don't ban them, on the basis that they assist navigation. But just because a GPS is legal doesn't mean that it does not increase the already considerable dangers of teen driving.

Finally, we should not neglect interference with hearing as a form of distracted driving. As iPads, smartphones, and similar devices have proliferated, it has become common to see drivers, especially younger ones, wearing earphones or headphones while they are driving, either the small plastic or rubber pieces that approximate the size of the inner part of the ear, or full-blown headgear that not only provides sound but is designed to block out most background noise. I really didn't think about the implications of this until I saw a young lady who was oblivious to an ambulance behind her, siren blaring, because she was listening to her iPod with earphones. In early 2012, two teen drivers died in two separate accidents when wearing headphones contributed to their not hearing an oncoming train at a rail crossing. The danger is real. Ears are essential safety equipment that should not be blocked.

According to AAA's Digest of State Motor Vehicle Laws, only a few states expressly regulate or prohibit the use of headphones while driving. In fact, most distracted driving laws specifically exempt "audio," and using an iPod or a similar device with earphones or headphones to play music, receive language instruction, listen to a book on tape, and so forth appears to be perfectly legal. Being hearing-impaired is not a reason that one cannot obtain a driver's license, and in fact there are programs to help drivers who have biological hearing loss cope with their condition.

But shouldn't driving with earphones or headphones be recognized as a dangerous form of distracted driving and treated as such, for teen drivers if not everyone? First of all, try putting on a good pair of headphones, the type that fit completely over your ears and are designed to block out all other sounds. They are very effective (and block out far more sound than just the audio system in a car played at high volume). Next consider how music played at a moderate or high volume further blocks any outside noise. *The ability to hear is an essential part of crash avoidance, and thus driving while wearing headphones decreases reaction time.* I am sure that any experienced driver can recall numerous circumstances where a siren, a crash, a bang, or some other noise was his first alert to a dangerous situation, perhaps even his only key in avoiding a crash.

For parents of teen drivers, then, this simple, obvious, and important caution: don't let your teen drivers wear earphones or headphones while they are driving. Purposely blocking off hearing while driving is plainly a bad idea. Reduction or loss of hearing is a form of distracted driving because it reduces reaction time to circumstances that can cause a crash or allow for crash avoidance. And note that, with regard to this form of distraction, parents may not have state laws to back them up; they are often on their own in imposing this limitation.

Teen drivers should be all ears, and parents should make sure they are.

19

Impaired Driving: Alcohol, Drugs, and Fatigue

Impaired driving is, first and foremost, distinct from distracted driving. When we discuss distraction, we are assuming an awake, alert teen driver whose concentration, judgment, coordination, and reaction time are all as good as they can physically and mentally be. A distraction, then, whether a text message, the conduct of a passenger, or something outside the car, is a momentary interruption of the driver's attention to the traffic situation. Impaired driving, on the other hand, is a physical or mental condition that continuously—for hours at a time—slows or otherwise interferes with mental and therefore physical responses to the driving situation. Thus, sleep deprivation, intoxication, or being under the influence of drugs directly elevate the risks of driving, not only because they interfere with a driver's ability to take the three steps necessary to avoid a crash (recognition/responsive action/redirecting or stopping the car) but also because the driver cannot recover these functions with a simple action such as turning off the cell phone.

Sleep deprivation and fatigue, of course, are difficult to supervise. It is well known that teens need more sleep than adults; for example, high schools across the country have been adjusting their starting times as science has documented this reality. A sleepy teen is hardly unusual. There are, of course, no laws requiring teen drivers to have gotten a specified amount of rest before driving. Except for an incidental benefit from nighttime restrictions, graduated driver licensing laws don't help with fatigue. *As a result, sufficient sleep is probably the single most important characteristic of teen drivers that parents and supervising adults must reevaluate every day—and perhaps even twice per day.* This is the area in which parents are most frequently called upon to make judgment calls based on facts that may not be clear (and short-term energy drinks are not the answer).

Drugs are the in-between category, because in addition to illegal drugs, millions of teens today take a wide variety of medications, all perfectly legal and often prescribed but whose impact on driving ability may be helpful, neutral, or harmful. A stimulant, arguably, could make a driver more alert, while a sedative might lower a driver's anxiety. Perhaps the most that can be said about drugs is that parents and supervising adults should carefully evaluate, with a doctor's help, the potential effects of prescriptions or over-the-counter medications on driving, and have zero tolerance for use of illegal drugs while driving.

Regarding alcohol, the good news is that public education and awareness are light-years ahead of where they were even a decade ago. In 2012, the Centers for Disease Control and Prevention reported that the percentage of teens driving under the influence of alcohol in 2011 was half (10 percent, down from 20 percent) of what it was in 1991. (However, part of this "progress" is the result of teens in 2011 driving less because of the high cost of gasoline.) The bad news: 30 percent of teen driver deaths are still alcohol related, with about 70 percent of these fatalities being boys. Also, at 10 percent, that's still more than one million teens drinking and driving.

For underage drinking prevention, I can do no better than to recommend Mothers Against Drunk Driving's Power of Parents program, which provides parents the research-based tools to talk with their teens about alcohol. You can learn more about the program at madd.org/powerofparents.

Otherwise, I can convey a list of best practices:

- make sure your teen knows that it is illegal for anyone under the age of twenty-one to drink and that it is illegal for teens to drink and drive;

- understand that, just as with driving habits, in your alcohol and drug use, you are modeling conduct for your teen;

- be in close contact with other parents or adults who are supervising your teen, or should be;

- when negotiating and signing a teen driving agreement, spend time on the zero tolerance paragraph about alcohol and drug use;

- regarding fatigue, make it clear that the provision allowing parents to make "override" calls to prohibit driving on a day-by-day basis applies particularly to your judgment about whether your teen has had sufficient rest;

- discuss with your teen the technique for getting out of a car being driven by an impaired driver, such as "Please pull over and let me out, I'm about to throw up"; and

- as stated in my model teen driving agreement, note specially for your teen the paragraph which says that "At any time and for any reason, I may call for a safe ride to avoid a dangerous situation," and "My reasons for requesting the ride will not be a violation of this agreement."

The challenges of alcohol, drugs, and fatigue are inextricably woven into numerous aspects of parenting, but the stakes are higher when the conduct at issue is driving drunk, high, or drowsy.

What Schools Can Do

While many parents may assume that late night and bad weather driving are the most hazardous times for teen drivers, there is a body of research showing that it is actually the hours directly after school lets out that are perilous, if not the most dangerous. If we think about it, this makes sense. Teens leaving school parking lots are the ones most likely to have illegal and distracting passengers; to be in a big hurry; to be headed to a destination (friend's house, fast food restaurant, and so on) that disqualifies the trip as "purposeful" driving. Teens leaving school may also be fatigued.

If this phenomenon is true, then the exit or exits from a high school's parking lot can be regarded as a type of Ground Zero for safe teen driving, a place at which time and effort spent on awareness and enforcement will pay dividends in safety. So what can schools do to use parking lot exits as a type of control point for teen drivers?

One technique is signage. Not just the familiar "Buckle Up" but signs that convey a more pointed message. The best I have heard about is a series of four signs, large enough so teen drivers can't miss or ignore them, that convey these messages in this order:

> **Ready to drive—no distractions?**

> **No illegal passengers?**

> **Seat belts buckled?**

> **Great!** *See you tomorrow.*

If a school's budget does not have funds for signs like these, a PTA or even a shop class or service organization can step up.

Another technique is spot checks of cars leaving the parking lot. This could be a formal roadblock set up by police or a community relations officer, but it also could be done by a student group, PTA, or parent volunteers. The intercepting can involve just a warning to violators, especially with respect to passengers, but if the school is serious about compliance, the program can also involve writing down and reporting license plates of violators and then taking some kind of enforcement action—losing a parking sticker or some in-school privilege for a period of time, for instance.

Surveillance cameras are another option. Many cities and towns, of course, are now installing such cameras at critical traffic locations to give drivers the message that violations will be recorded and prosecuted. Why not school parking lots? The danger is documented, so the cost should be justifiable.

I recently attended a meeting of driving school owners at which one pointed out that teen drivers leaving school parking lots are most likely to have illegal passengers on unexpected early dismissal days, such as when a snowstorm is approaching. On these days, parents, guardians, and others who are responsible for transporting teens home may not be able to make it, so teens grab a ride, whether legal and safe or not, with whoever can get them home quickest. Perhaps each school announcement about early dismissal should be accompanied by a reminder that rushing home to beat a storm is not a reason to violate safe teen driving/passenger laws.

Schools and parent organizations can also help by encouraging and facilitating carpools with parent drivers specifically as a way to prevent risky teen driving with passengers. After transporting kids to school, often in carpools, or putting them on a bus from kindergarten on, parents almost subconsciously yield to allowing peers to take over. Undoubtedly, the convenience (and perhaps more sleep) for parents spurs this along. But parents should realize that they are not required to give up this role, and they can take it back immediately to avoid higher-risk situations such as bad weather or night transportation. The convenience of having teens drive should not take the place of parent-initiated carpools if that is the safer option.

What else can schools do to promote safer teen driving? The National Organizations for Youth Safety (NOYS; www.noys.org) promotes several innovative programs, among them Act Out Loud and Grim Reaper Day. Other ideas include:

- forming a student-parent-faculty safe teen driving awareness group;
- broadcasting safe teen driving public service announcements over the intercom/PA system;
- sponsoring a schoolwide video or poster contest;
- hanging a safe teen driving banner in a strategic location;
- hosting a Safe Teen Driver Night with representatives from emergency medical services and law enforcement;
- holding an annual Safe Teen Driving Awareness Day;
- incorporating safe teen driving into the school's health or wellness curriculum;
- inviting guest speakers who can tell riveting personal stories (see chapter 11, the description of Mourning Parents Act); and
- conducting an essay contest in a school publication.

Discussed above are proactive steps that schools can take, but there is one other long-standing practice that schools should change.

Every summer, most high schools send forms to parents and guardians that ask them for permission with respect to transporting students to and from school activities. The forms usually look something like this:

☐ Yes ☐ No   I give permission for my student to drive to and from school.

☐ Yes ☐ No   I give permission for my student to ride to off-campus events/activities with other students as drivers.

☐ Yes ☐ No   I give permission for my student to drive other students to off-campus events/activities.

This is usually the total extent of the forms, though sometimes they also ask if the student is authorized to drive a sibling to school, and sometimes they ask the parent/guardian to verify that the car the student will drive is insured.

These forms are a multipart invitation to trouble because:

- the most dangerous hours for teen drivers are the hours directly after school lets out;

- these "Yes/No" forms, if checked yes, allow your teen driver, with the school's blessing, to ride as a passenger with a driver unknown to you, and perhaps with other students in the car;

- they rarely make any reference to the state's teen driving law and passenger restrictions;

- they can give the impression that off-campus events/activities are an exception to teen driver laws and passenger restrictions; and

- these forms not only encourage but authorize a practice that we know is dangerous, teens driving with passengers.

Why do schools use these forms? To save money on transportation and gas, no doubt. Perhaps also because the same form has been used for decades. Why do parents check yes? Well, the forms come from the school, so someone must have decided that students driving other students is safe, right?

In fairness, there is one aspect of the driving authorized by these forms that actually carries a lower risk. Most likely, one student transporting others would be "purposeful" driving. But this is the only counterweight to an otherwise dangerous practice.

What should schools and parents do? The safest option would be to not allow high school students to drive other students to school events, period. If transportation is needed, buses should be used or parents/guardians should be the drivers. Barring this complete prohibition, schools can:

- remind parents on the forms themselves what the state's passenger rules are (for example, "Our state prohibits teen drivers from carrying non–family members as passengers for one year after licensing");

- remind students and parents on a case-by-case, event-by-event basis when their transportation to and from a school event will involve a teen driver;

- ask coaches and other supervisors of activities such as sports practices that occur before or after school, or when school is not in session, to make sure they "hand off" their students to a safe ride home;

- bar any teen who has received a ticket, citation, or license suspension from driving other students (which, of course, requires the teen or parents to notify the school);

- have each teen driver sign a school version of a teen driver agreement, committing to safe practices such as no electronic devices when transporting students; and

- remind every student who will be a passenger of a student driver of the importance of a distraction-free car and use of safety belts, and if the driver engages in unsafe driving, getting out of the car.

Lastly, schools can play a role in conveying information about their students. Businesses, governments, and schools have long understood that one way to boost compliance is to shine a spotlight, to either publicize a list of who has followed the rules (positive reinforcement) or make violators known. Businesses post the names of employees with perfect attendance records. Governments publish the roll of who is behind on property tax payments. Schools print their honor rolls in local newspapers. Newspapers reprint police blotters. Public recognition is an incentive to do the right thing, while public reckoning can be a powerful deterrent.

Back in the good old days—the 1990s and before—the locations for such publicity at schools were newspapers and bulletin boards, but in recent years, of course, the practice has migrated to websites. Most high schools in the United States have at least a modest website. Why then can't we use school websites to help promote safer teen driving? Websites can announce and promote each of the safe driving events listed above. My suggestion here, however, envisions a step beyond merely informational messages: using the website to shine a spotlight on each student who has had his or her license long enough to carry passengers legally.

What about the administrative burden of collecting and maintaining this list? Yes, it will probably take someone on staff a few hours to coordinate with parents and students to compile the initial list and a few minutes now and then to update it, but I doubt that the time required will be significant, and in any event, the safety benefit and greater peace of mind should make it worthwhile. Moreover, I suspect that students and maybe even parents will consider adding their names to a list of this type to be a minigraduation of sorts, an announcement that Teen A has climbed another step toward adulthood. Thus, all the school may need to do is establish the list and explain how to add or delete a name and the date on which the student became eligible to carry passengers.

Dedicating a small corner of a school website to a list of drivers who can carry passengers and so far have been safe drivers will not be a cure-all. In particular, simply because Student A has now had a full license long enough to carry passengers and has managed this initial period without a violation does not, by any measure, ensure that we now have a reliably safe or experienced driver. The goal would be to provide one more resource to help parents make better decisions about when their teens should get behind the wheel or should get into a car when a teen will be behind the wheel.

Blind Zones

A teen, at home, suddenly realizes that she is late—for school, sports, an activity, a community event, a family gathering, a date, whatever. She races into the kitchen, grabs the car keys from the basket, jumps into the car, starts the engine, and starts backing down the driveway.

And doesn't look to see if anything or anyone is behind the vehicle, and so doesn't see the toddler playing in the driveway.

This stomach-turning scenario is not too difficult to envision, is it?

Every week in the United States, at least fifty children are backed over by vehicles because they could not be seen by the driver. In some cases, the driver carefully checked the blind zones before getting into the vehicle but then a toddler wandered into the zone just as the car started rolling. In other words, not every back-over is the result of carelessness, but all are a result of the fact that there are places that drivers cannot see.

Educating the public about blind zones is part of the mission of KidsAndCars, www.KidsAndCars.org, based in Kansas. Blind zones are essential information for teen drivers, though of course the rest of us need to be reminded of them also. Blind zones are one of those safety risks, that, I think, lie just below the surface of our consciousness as drivers and parents, and so reminders are critical.

The KidsAndCars website has photos and illustrations of the danger. Every vehicle has blind zones in front of and behind the vehicle, with a bigger blind zone behind. The exact length, width, and height of the zone varies with the height of the driver, the height of the driver's seat, and the nature of the vehicle, but the area can be anywhere from twenty to sixty feet long. Obviously, SUVs, light trucks, and cars with low suspensions have the biggest potential blind zones. In recent years, the number of blind zone incidents has increased dramatically, which I assume is the result of more SUVs and light trucks being driven by the American public. The KidsAndCars website has the frightening statistics.

Technology is becoming part of the answer here. Some new cars have a backup camera, and it is expected that such cameras will become standard on most cars in the next several years. Older vehicles can be retrofitted with backup cameras. However, even the backup camera doesn't see everything, and the device can also distract the driver from checking the other sides of the vehicle.

There is no magic solution here. Explain to your teen what a blind zone is, and point out approximately how large it is in the front and rear of each car your teen may drive. Then direct your teen to the KidsAndCars website to view the illustrations and to read some of the horror stories of drivers who started their vehicles rolling without checking the blind zone.

22

Vehicle Identification Stickers

A hotly debated topic in teen driver safety is a system by which law enforcement and other drivers may identify a vehicle being driven by a teen. The system already exists, in the sense that driver's ed cars usually carry a "Student Driver" sign. The debated idea is to have teens display a similar sticker somewhere on or within the vehicle when they are not being supervised by a driving instructor. The United Kingdom, for one, has done this for years, requiring new drivers to display an "L" (for Learner) in the rear window.

In the United States, only New Jersey has adopted this system, because pushback from parents is substantial. The most common arguments are that displaying a sticker may lead a sexual predator to target a solo teen driver, especially a girl, and may induce law enforcement to profile and take action based solely on the age of the driver. The principal counterargument is that police should be not only allowed but also encouraged to spotlight teen drivers because of their high crash rates, and that teen drivers will drive more responsibly if they know that law enforcement officials are capable of identifying their vehicles. (One compromise suggestion is to embed in the license plates or rear windows of cars driven by teens a sensor that can be detected only by law enforcement—a technology that is technically feasible but to my knowledge not yet implemented in any state.)

New Jersey's first two years of experimentation with a decal system have been successful: crash rates have declined, law enforcement officers have embraced the extra enforcement tool, and predators targeting teens has not been a problem. Nonetheless, opposition among parents and teens has persisted, and some have ignored the requirement.

It is undeniably true that teen driver laws are difficult for police to enforce if they can't identify vehicles driven by teens. Indeed, it is an anomaly that GDL laws are passed to impose special rules based on the age of the driver, but law enforcement has no way to detect which vehicles are subject to these rules. Does it make sense that we identify student drivers when they are in the car with an instructor but not when they drive by themselves or without a supervising adult? With the results from New Jersey now part of the mix, the debate continues.

23

Simulators and High-Performance Driving Schools

Two ways that are sometimes used to supplement a teen driver's actual behind-the-wheel training time are simulators (sometimes also known as virtual reality training) and high-performance driving programs (also known as "skid schools"). If we conceive of driving as the experience of reacting correctly to the complex and rapidly changing circumstances of maneuvering a car through traffic and the vehicles, signs, signals, structures, barriers, pedestrians, and weather that drivers routinely encounter, then the purpose of a simulator is to improve a driver's reactions.

High-performance driving schools, in what television advertisements call a "closed course" or "closed environment," teach reactions to sudden or emergency situations such as taking evasive action to avoid a crash or turning the wheel and using the brakes to counteract a skid. In particular, high-performance schools allow drivers to practice emergency response in a way and in a place that generally can't be replicated by a parent or even a driver's ed instructor.

Parents should be forewarned of several facts about each type of training. Skid control practice and simulators may give teen drivers a false sense of security, a feeling that they can now drive faster, take turns more sharply, or otherwise push the envelope of vehicle controls *because* they have received extra training about how to react in a potential crash situation. Several studies have shown that so-called advanced skill training for teens actually increases crash rates. High-performance driving practice can be exhilarating—not what we want for a new driver. Most experts I have talked to say that what teens most need are defensive driving skills and the confidence to look beyond the perimeter of their own vehicle to the traffic situation ahead. Simulators and high-performance classes don't provide these types of training.

Non-English-
Speaking and Single
Parent Households

The problem of conveying health and safety information to non-English-speaking households is an enormous one, and it reaches far beyond safe teen driving. I can only summarize the basic elements of the problem. To convey safety warnings effectively, messages must be not only in the listener's language but also in the correct dialect, and delivered in a culturally relevant manner. As but one example, in some cultures a predominant belief is that an individual has little control over life's occurrences. Such an attitude could undermine a take-charge message to parents of new drivers.

Single parent households can also present a unique challenge, illustrated by this story. A mother, divorced for several years from the father of her newly licensed sixteen-year-old daughter, asked me what to do when her ex-husband bought their daughter a car. These parents live in the same region and are in regular communication, but the father did not ask for the mother's consent before buying this car.

I offered the mother two pieces of advice. The first was to bring to her ex-husband's attention the recent State Farm/Children's Hospital of Philadelphia study showing that teen drivers with their own cars have higher crash rates than those who depend on shared cars (chapter 17). Second, I suggested that the mother download a teen driving agreement and that all three of them discuss it, agree on it, and sign it ASAP.

Though her driving between each parent's home might be considered "purposeful," the car purchase likely forced the daughter into more driving than she was ready to handle. Also, the non-custodial parent surprising the other parent by buying a car for their new teen driver raises a question about which parent is overseeing driving privileges and safety. Finally, it would seem that in this situation, the father might be characterized as at least one parent putting convenience ahead of safety.

This family's circumstances call for even greater caution and conversation, with decisions about the daughter's driving to be made day by day and on a case-by-case basis. A teen driving agreement signed by both parents would be a good start.

25

Supervising Other People's Teens

You observe a teen driver you know—from school, sports, a community activity, the neighborhood—speeding, texting, drag racing, carrying passengers you know are illegal, or driving after the state's curfew. Do you inform the teen driver's parent or guardian?

Your own teen reports seeing others at her school leaving the parking lot with passengers whose presence violates the state's passenger restrictions. She also knows this group is going to be unruly and dangerous. Should she inform someone at the school? Should you?

When it comes to teen drivers, are parents keepers of other people's kids?

The fears that a parent would have in calling the parent of a teen driver who was observed driving illegally or dangerously are easy to catalogue. To begin with, there is the likely problem that the parent of that teen does not understand, or does not want to understand, the dangers of teen driving, and so will respond to your "I saw Billy texting while driving" message with an out loud or internal "Yeah, so what?" The parent may respond with a stern warning to "mind your own business," or perhaps a snotty question about whether your own driving or your teen's driving are so perfect that you have now been appointed community watchdog (or God). Maybe the parent on the receiving end will get defensive because the driving conduct you describe is something this parent does routinely, so your comment is a complaint about not only the teen's driving, but also the parent's. And in these days of tweets and electronic messages that ricochet around town and beyond in seconds, one may fear that a complaint about another parent's teen driver will end up as a post on Facebook or a tweet on Twitter, and what started out as a well-intentioned, one-to-one alert will suddenly have you facing town-wide ridicule as a goody-two-shoes or a tattletale.

Yes, it is easy to list the reasons why you shouldn't even consider being an informant about another family's teen driver. Yet there are just as many reasons why you should.

The starting point is the recognition that safe teen driving is everyone's concern, for the simple and well-documented reason that teen drivers crash three times more frequently than the safest age group of drivers, the thirty-five- to forty-nine-year-olds; and when they do, they injure or kill many more people than themselves. Every year in our country, three million teens get their licenses; they share the road with us. The safety of every driver and passenger is more in jeopardy with teen drivers than with any other age group. And this is before we factor in texting.

Next, please ask yourself: If your teen driver was doing something dangerous, would you want to be informed, regardless of the source? Hopefully your quick and unhesitating answer is yes.

Let's also remember that the police simply cannot be everywhere, or even most places we need them, so supervision of teen drivers is primarily up to parents. To say that this responsibility is limited to your own teen driver is to draw an unnecessary line and to open up a gap in the supervision that is essential to safe teen driving.

Finally, please note that with teen drivers, time is the enemy. If teen drivers misbehave and get away with it, they are empowered to act the same way again, or even to push the envelope further. It is well documented that teen driver attitudes deteriorate in the first six months after they obtain their licenses (chapter 15), when the lessons and cautions of driver's ed and the learner's permit stage are easily forgotten and the inherent teen attraction to risk-taking kicks in. Bad or illegal driving observed but not reported is not just an omission but a refusal to take a step that is important to public safety.

Everything considered, a prompt report to a parent, guardian, school official, or whoever is best situated to act on information about teen driver misconduct, is a responsibility that each of us has to the safety of our families, our communities, and ourselves.

This leaves us with two issues: how best to communicate, and what to say? As to how to do it, the options are face-to-face conversation, a phone call, or an e-mail or text message. This is a judgment call. The problem with an e-mail or text, of course, is that it may get forwarded somewhere that you can't control and don't want it to be, and this may be a deterrent ("Look at what this guy said about my Alice!"). A face-to-face visit may compress the fears listed above. A phone call may be the safest way.

Were it up to me to call another parent to report on a teen driver doing something illegal or dangerous, I would strive to use a script something like this:

> This is Tim from Jones Road. I want to apologize in advance for this call and hope you will understand why I am calling. I saw your daughter texting while driving on Hope Street. It made me very concerned for her safety and those driving nearby. [Here, one can insert a compliment about the teen: "She is such a great young lady."] Again, I hope you're not offended by my bringing this up. I'm doing this out of concern for safety. I appreciate your taking my call.

At the risk of using a cliché, when it comes to safe teen driving, it definitely takes a village. So please, don't be afraid to call, and don't delay.

26

In Summary:
Tips from Reid's Dad,
www.fromreidsdad.org

1. Keep in mind that there is no such thing as a safe teen driver, primarily because the part of the human brain that provides judgment and restraint does not fully develop until ages twenty-two to twenty-five, and no amount of training can overcome this limitation.

2. Remember that a graduate of driver's ed is a beginner, not a safe or experienced driver.

3. Recognize that enforcement of teen driving laws is primarily up to supervising adults; police and schools can only help.

4. Make handing over car keys a big-deal ceremony, every time.

5. Don't push a teen who, for whatever reason, is not ready to drive safely.

6. Prepare and sign a teen driving agreement, and enforce it.

7. Recognize the factors that substantially increase the already-high risk of a teen driver getting in a crash: speeding, drugs and alcohol, fatigue, bad weather, or an unsafe vehicle.

8. Recognize the difference between "purposeful" and "recreational" driving.

9. Understand that each passenger in a teen's car increases the likelihood of a crash, including siblings.

10. Demand full seat belt compliance by every teen driver and every passenger.

11. Recognize the first six months of solo driving as the most dangerous.

12. Don't let a teen be the primary or only driver of a car, and in any event, choose a car with the most safety features.

13. Be aware of the most dangerous times for teen drivers: after school lets out, 9:00 PM to midnight, and summer.

14. If a teen receives a ticket or citation, make her take her medicine without argument or delay.

15. Have zero tolerance for a teen driver using an electronic device, including a GPS, to text, type, read, watch video, or make a phone call.

16. Don't allow your teen to wear headphones while driving.

17. Beware school transportation forms that allow teens to carry passengers.

18. If you can afford one of the technologies that track your teen's driving, buy and install it.

19. Be responsible for all teen drivers you come in contact with, not just yours.

20. Don't put your convenience ahead of a teen driver's safety.

21. Be a good role model: avoid distractions, buckle up, obey speed limits, and be a defensive driver.

AFTERWORD

A Plea to Parents

I began this book with the true statement that, in the weeks and months after Reid's crash, I was "less haunted by the feeling that I had made a terrible mistake in supervising my son's driving and more confused by the sense that I had done what parents are supposed to do—and he still died." I thought I was a reasonably well-informed, hands-on, mainstream parent.

I wasn't. Not even close. As chapter 1 ("My Story") reveals, I made plenty of mistakes, because—like too many parents—I did not understand the dangers or the steps I could take to counteract them. I thought driver's ed had made Reid a relatively safe driver, and that getting his license from our DMV was further confirmation. I didn't act like an air traffic controller. We didn't sign a teen driving agreement. I allowed him to buy his own car, and then to take it to "hang" with his friends. I signed a form allowing him to drive others to and from school activities. I didn't understand the dangers of cell phones or texting.

In my defense, he drove a relatively safe car crash-free for eleven months, and on the night he died, he took the car on an unauthorized joyride with passengers. Alcohol, drugs, fatigue, his cell phone, and his passengers played no role in his crash, and it's a fact that an eighteen-inch change in where his car hit the guardrail would have spared his life when speed and inexperience caused him to lose control.

I don't beat myself up anymore about what happened. I didn't give him the keys on the night of December 1, 2006. I didn't OK his route or passengers, and no parent can supervise a teen driver 24/7. Occasionally I count my blessings: Reid's crash didn't kill anyone else.

I am left to convey this message to parents: Be better than I was. Learn from my experience and homework, and resolve to avoid my mistakes.

I realize that the core challenge of parenting teens is balancing exposure to risk with protection. We want them to learn, to explore opportunities reachable only or best by car. Driving is part of growing up, and who wants to delay that?

But please:

- Use utmost caution.

- Understand how unalterably dangerous teen driving is.

- Don't put convenience ahead of safety.

- Be proactive day by day.

- Preempt the riskiest situations.

- Let the tether out in very small increments.

- If your gut says that a particular drive is a bad idea, go with your instinct, not peer pressure.

- Don't befriend your teen with car keys.

The consequences of a teen driver fatality or serious injury are beyond the scope of this book, but trust me, the emotional pain is beyond your imagination. This book's advice is not a guarantee of safety, but its steps are proven ways for you and your family to better manage the risks of teen driving and avoid the unthinkable.

Thanks for listening.

—Tim

TEEN DRIVING RESOURCES

www.allstate.com/foundation/teen-safe-driving.aspx—Website of the Allstate Foundation; Allstate has mounted a national campaign to promote the use of parent-teen driver agreements.

www.aaafoundation.org—Website of American Automobile Association Foundation, which includes in-depth research on teen driving and instruction

www.cdc.gov/features/safeteendriving—Centers for Disease Control and Prevention's teen driving website

www.childrenshospitalblog.org—Children's health blog by Children's Hospital in Boston

www.teendriversource.org—Website of Children's Hospital of Philadelphia, a national leader in safe teen driving research

www.distraction.gov—US Department of Transportation website that summarizes current research about distracted driving

www.drivingskillsforlife.com—Ford's Driving Skills for Life program

www.impactteendrivers.org—A Sacramento, California–based coalition of parents, law enforcement, and first responders that provides innovative training programs

www.iihs.org—The Insurance Institute for Highway Safety, a national leader in researching all aspects of traffic safety

www.libertymutual.com/teendriving—Website of Liberty Mutual Insurance, offering parent and teen tips and tools. Through a partnership with SADD, Liberty Mutual regularly publishes original research into teen and family attitudes and behaviors concerning teen driving and underage drinking.

www.lifesaversconference.org—Website of the annual national meeting of traffic safety professionals

www.madd.org/powerofparents—MADD's underage drinking prevention program, which includes a specific section on teen driving

www.mourningparentsact.org—A Connecticut-based organization of parents who have lost children in automobile accidents (I am a participant); the group brings a message, in person, to high school students about the consequences for families of unsafe driving.

www.nhtsa.dot.gov—The National Highway Traffic Safety Administration, a federal agency; the "Teen Driving" portion of its website has a trove of information, resources, and statistics for parents.

www.noys.org—National Organizations for Youth Safety (NOYS), a national coalition of groups whose mission involves all aspects of youth safety and safe teen driving in particular. NOYS has been very active recently in combating texting and distracted driving among teen drivers. "Under Your Influence," www.underyourinfluence.org, is its specific safe teen driving monthly e-newsletter.

www.nsc.org/safety_home/MotorVehicleSafety/Pages/Motor VehicleSafety.aspx—National Safety Council, which publishes *Teen Driver: A Family Guide to Teen Driver Safety* (2004)

www.sadd.org—Website of Students Against Destructive Decisions, which includes educational and prevention materials for students to use in their schools and communities, as well as information for parents, teachers, and other caring adults

www.safercar.gov—US government's comprehensive list of vehicle safety ratings

www.betterteendriving.com—Website of the State Farm Insurance Company

www.toyotadrivingexpectations.com—Toyota's teen driver program

Model Teen Driving Agreement

Cautions for Supervising Adults

- Parents may prohibit those under eighteen from starting to drive. *Review the safety risks and use your judgment.*
- Teen drivers *should not use any electronic device*, at any time that the vehicle is not in Park, *to text, type, read, watch video, or communicate with someone outside the vehicle.*
- You are a *role model for your teen*, and need to be a safe, responsible, defensive driver.

Safety Risks

INITIALS   *(teen and supervising adult(s) to initial each)*

_____ Driving is especially dangerous for teens because the human brain does not fully develop its ability to assess risk and danger or control impulse until the mid-twenties. No amount of teen driver training can overcome this limitation.

_____ Passing a driver training course and obtaining a driver's license means that a teen is a beginner, not a safe driver.

_____ A teen driver can cause injury, death, and damage, which can result in criminal and civil penalties and financial liability for parents.

_____ Reckless driving risks the life of the driver, passengers, other drivers, and pedestrians.

Teen Driver Agreement

1. Time Period: This Agreement will remain in effect until *(recommended: one year or eighteenth birthday, whichever is later)* _____.

2. Supervising Adult: My driving will be supervised by one or more adults who will decide, day by day, whether it is safe for me to drive.

3. Driving Plan: I will get permission from one of my supervising adults every time I drive, and we will agree on my route, destination, time of return, and passengers. Joyriding (driving with no destination or purpose) is not allowed.

4. Seat Belts: I will wear my seat belt and I will make sure that every passenger in my car wears one.

5. Electronic Devices: Unless my vehicle is in Park, I will not use any electronic device, even hands-free, to text, type, read, watch video, or communicate with a person outside the vehicle.

6. Curfews: I understand that I may not drive between the hours of *(fill in state curfew, or stricter hours)* _____, except for *(fill in state law exceptions)* _____. If I need extended time (as for a job or school activity), I will get written permission and carry it in my vehicle.

7. Passengers *(must be consistent with state law; may be stricter; recommend three stages)*: For my first _____ months with a license, I will carry only an adult who is supervising my driving. In the next _____ months, I will carry only a supervising driver and immediate family. I will not transport anyone else until I have had my license for *(recommend one year)* _____.

8. Alcohol or Drug Use, Fatigue: I will never drive under the influence or alcohol or drugs, or when I have not had sufficient rest.

9. Speeding: I will obey speed limits, stop signs, traffic signals, and the rules of the road. I will adjust my speed based on road conditions (*i.e.*, weather, turns, hills, visibility, unfamiliar roads).

10. Suspension of Driving Privileges: Violations of this Agreement or state laws may be reported to one of my supervising adults by law enforcement, neighbors, school personnel, or friends. *IF I VIOLATE ANY OF THESE OBLIGATIONS, MY DRIVING PRIVILEGES WILL BE SUSPENDED FOR _____ DAYS.* This suspension will be in addition to state law requirements. If I drive while my privileges are suspended, they will be suspended indefinitely.

11. Call for Safe Ride: At any time, I may call for a safe ride to avoid a dangerous situation. My reasons for requesting the ride will not be a violation of this Agreement.

12. Finances: During this Agreement, costs of insurance, gas, and maintenance will be divided: _____.

13. Technology: *(Specify any device that will be installed or used to track information about the teen's operation of the vehicle.)* _____.

14. Mediator *(optional)*: We appoint _____ to serve as mediator. If a dispute arises about this Agreement, we will ask our mediator for advice.

BY SIGNING, WE COMMIT OURSELVES TO THE REQUIREMENTS OF THIS AGREEMENT.

ACKNOWLEDGMENTS

In 2006, I would have given everything I have to save my son and avoid the pain that followed his passing. But counting my blessings, I gratefully acknowledge the people without whom this book would not have been written.

First and foremost, thanks to my wife Ellen and my daughter Martha for being my cheerleaders and advisers.

This book was originally the suggestion of my college classmate and publishing industry veteran Kathy Mintz. She saw before I did that my blog had accumulated enough content and national interest to warrant a handbook. Matt Richtel of the *New York Times* provided specific inspiration, and the belief that I could make a difference, through his 2009–10 Pulitzer Prize–winning series on distracted driving.

My gratitude to Sandy Spavone and Nicole Graziosi of the National Organizations for Youth Safety is difficult to express. In early 2011, they embraced this project and have energetically supported it since. NOYS has done as much for the well-being of the youth of America as any organization, and it has been my honor to be part of their work.

Curt Clarisey of Simsbury, Connecticut, designed my blog and has faithfully maintained and improved it. He educated me about successful blogging. Curt, thank you for your tireless efforts.

Joy Tutela has been so much more than my agent: friend, confidante, adviser, and rock. Her unwavering belief in Reid's story as a way to help parents has kept me going.

It has been a joy to work with the folks at Chicago Review Press/ Independent Publishers Group, including editor Lisa Reardon, as well as Jen Wisnowski, Amelia Estrich, and Mary Kravenas.

My assistant of twenty years, Erin Fitzgerald, has typed and formatted countless revisions of this manuscript, and has done so always with her ever-present cheerfulness.

Thanks to Attorney Robert Labate for his help with legal matters.

Cathy Gillen of PTG Enterprises graciously allowed me to benefit from her incomparable knowledge and contacts in the traffic safety and transportation communities.

Thank you to those in the national and New England automotive and traffic safety communities who edited or commented on the manuscript: Kevin Borrup and Garry Lapidus of Connecticut Children's Medical Center; Dr. Kelly Browning of California's Impact Teen Drivers; Sharon Silke Carty of the *Huffington Post*; Sherry Chapman of !MPACT; Pam Fischer, New Jersey parent and advocate; Cathy Gillen of the Road Safety Foundation; Bruce Hamilton of AAA Foundation; Dean Johnson of the Sandy Wood Johnson Foundation; Rik Paul of *Consumer Reports*; Karen Polan of Toyota; Dave Preusser of Preusser Research Group; and Piña Violano of Yale-New Haven Hospital.

Thank you to the Marketing Department staff at Shipman & Goodwin LLP, Jill Mastrianni, Jen Stokes, and Maria Ramsay for their belief in my mission and expert support for my safe teen driving presentations. Thanks also to Shipman & Goodwin colleagues, Scott Murphy and Barry Hawkins especially, for giving me encouragement and time to work on safe teen driving, and to support staff Jeanne Swayner, Carolyn Lawrence, Deanna Alvarez, and Jessie Rodriguez for their tireless evening and weekend help.

In April 2013, a focus group drawn from attendees of the Lifesavers Conference on Highway Safety Priorities and ably led by Dr. Kelly Browning, provided invaluable feedback on the final draft of this book. Thank you to Mi Ae Lipe, Rosalie Ashcraft, Ted Beckman, Kathy Bernstein, Lee Boan, Sgt. Matt Cabot, Leeana Clegg, Amanda Foster, Howard Hedegard, Herbert Homan, Lisa Kutis, Lorrie Lynn, Pam Morrison, Susanne Ogaitis-Jones, Brian Pearse, Gordy Pehrson, Karen Pennington, David Resnick, Jackie Stackhouse Leach, Richard Sullivan, Margaret Skrzypkowski, Donna Tate, Dana Teramoto, and Stacey Tisdale.

Thank you, finally, to my new friends in the Connecticut and national traffic safety communities: Michelle Anderson, Liza Barth, Roy Bavaro, Ernie Bertothy, Angie Byrne, Dr. Brendan Campbell, Neal Chaudhary, Jenny Cheek, Hilda Crespo, Joe Cristalli, Commissioner Melody Currey, Mario Damiata, Diana Imondi Dias, Victor Diaz, Dr. Bella Dinh-Zarr, Brendan Dufor, Janette Fennell, Joel Feldman and Dianne Anderson, Ami Ghadia, Bob Green, Rep. Tony Guerrera, Shelley Hammond, Jack Hanley, Richard Hastings, Jim Hedlund, Suzanne Hill, Jack Hoch, Amy Hollingsworth, Donna Jenner, Julie Kettner, Peter Kissinger, Gary Knepler, Vicki Knox, Jill Konopka, Jim MacPherson, Laura and Vince Marchetti, Justin McNaull, Erin Meluso, Kelly Murphy, Susan Naide, Janice Palmer, Starrla Pennick, Juliet Pennington, Gordy Pehrson, Gov. M. Jodi Rell, Dave Roy, Bill Seymour, Marian Storch, Joe Toole, Lynn Townshend, Col. Paul Vance, Faith Voswinkel, Robert Ward, Penny Wells, and Bill Windsor. I am blessed many times over.

INDEX

ABOUT THE AUTHOR

Tim Hollister's seventeen-year-old son, Reid, died in a one-car crash on an interstate highway in central Connecticut in 2006. A year later, and after several other fatal crashes in the state, Connecticut's governor appointed Tim as a bereaved parent to a task force charged with reexamining the state's teen driver law. That task force led the state in 2008 to transform its law from one of the most lenient in the nation to one of the strictest. After serving on the task force, Tim began speaking and writing about topics largely unaddressed in the literature available to parents of teen drivers—what they can do before their teens get behind the wheel to preempt the most dangerous situations.

In 2009, Tim launched his national blog for parents of teen drivers, "From Reid's Dad," www.fromreidsddad.org. The blog has been featured on Kyra Phillips's *Raising America* on HLN and has been covered by the *Huffington Post*, television and radio stations, newspapers, newsletters, websites, and other

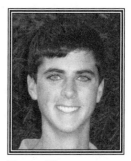

REID HOLLISTER
July 22, 1989–December 2, 2006

blogs and is now relied upon by parents, government agencies, driving schools, law enforcement, and traffic safety advocates across the country. In 2010 the National Highway Transportation Safety Administration honored Tim with its Public Service Award, the US Department of Transportation's highest civilian award for traffic safety.

Tim is a partner in a law firm, practicing land use and environmental law. For the past several years he has been listed among the *Best Lawyers in America*. He lives in Connecticut with his wife and daughter.